RADICAL PASSIVIT

RADICAL PASSIVITY

Levinas, Blanchot, and Agamben

Thomas Carl Wall

with a Foreword by William Flesch

STATE UNIVERSITY OF NEW YORK PRESS

Published by
State University of New York Press

© 1999 State University of New York

For information, address the State University of New York Press,
State University Plaza, Albany, NY 12246

Marketing by Anne Valentine
Production by Bernadine Dawes

Library of Congress Cataloging-in-Publication Data

Wall, Thomas Carl, 1954–
Radical passivity : Lévinas, Blanchot, and Agamben / Thomas Carl
Wall : with a foreword by William Flesch.
        p. cm.
Includes bibliographical references and index.
ISBN 0-7914-4047-8 (hardcover), — ISBN 0-7914-4048-6 (pbk.)
1. Lévinas, Emmanuel. 2. Blanchot, Maurice. 3. Agamben, Giorgio.
        1942–   . I. Title.
B2430.L484W35   1999   98–27843
111—DC21   CIP

1   2   3   4   5   6   7   8   9   10

For
Steven Shaviro
and
Mikkel Borch-Jacobsen

Contents

Love's Characters

Wallace Stevens, who loved Maurice Blanchot, in about 1955: "French and English constitute a single language." Blanchot himself (our own "extreme contemporary" as Leslie Hill calls him), a few years earlier: "A trop bon compte, un texte traduit mime l'effort de création qui, à partir de la langue courante, celle dans laquelle nous vivons et nous sommes immergés, cherche à faire naître une autre langue, en apparence la même et pourtant, par rapport à cette langue, comme son absence, sa différence perpétuellement acquise et constamment cachée." Such relatively facile translation is too easy a path to something that is nevertheless not easy, the way that in the literary work the writer will make language undergo "la transmutation qui d'une seule langue doit en tirer deux, l'une qui est lue et comprise sans détour, l'autre qui reste ignorée, tue et inaccessible et dont l'absence (l'ombre dont parle Tolstoï) est tout ce que nous en saisissons." It is this which Stevens is speaking of as well—the single language nameable only as two, French and English.

The ease with which translation can yield mock-profundity

has been a hazard for English language readers of Blanchot, Levinas, and Agamben (as has perhaps the native ease with which French and Italian speakers may read them). The stylistic infelicity of the English language for their kind of writing has not infrequently tended to yield in their followers a kind of empty sloganeering, a claim to some knowledge different from that great eerie clarity so essential to what they are saying. (That French is not Levinas's native language may put him in the position of the narrator in *L'Arrêt de mort,* responsive in a language whose responsibility cannot be a given.)

For years it has seemed to me, ever since reading Lydia Davis's supple and heroic attempts to render Blanchot in English (in a letter to Steven Shaviro Blanchot says of her, "Elle sait ce qu'il en est de traduire l'intraduisable"), that the only way for an English language reader to read Blanchot has been within that single language Stevens describes. The English we speak everyday had seemed too quirky for Blanchot. J. L. Austin suggests that we'll get somewhere in aesthetics when we stop trying to figure out the meaning of the beautiful and start looking to describe "the dainty and the dumpy" instead, and it has been the fundamentally comic genius of English as a literary language (even the English of Stevens), to marshal such categories of experience.

We would be tempted to call this *familiar* experience, Hume at billiards, Austen in Bath, Trollope at a hunt, experience whose description might be "read and understood directly." Blanchot's clarities seem something else, restrained without reticence, austere without haughtiness, careful without anxiety, fascinated without cathexis, impersonal without coldness. In Blanchot the name of such a state is love, a word used very rarely in his work, and only with the greatest diffidence. And yet what state is more familiar than love? Familiar to us and the channel of the familiar?

The channel of the familiar because you may use the second person familiar with the one you love: *tutoiement*. But perhaps one way to characterize Blanchot is to note the extreme demands he places on *tutoiement*. In his fictions his narrators consistently insist on its rarity. In his latest essay, "Pour l'amitié" Blanchot describes the atmosphere of May '68 as one in which *tutoiement* was demanded of everyone. It was only with his friends, and not with the comrades of those times, that Blanchot would use the formal "vous," sign of politeness to his friends, but more of his friendship, which could never use "tu" offhandedly. At the end of the essay Blanchot says that it is only Levinas whom he will "tutoyer," his friendship with Levinas, his friendship with his other friends, and his friendship with friendship demanding this distinctive, impersonal, unfamiliar, and uncanny formality with familiarity itself.

Freud calls the uncanny the return of the familiar and sees the fact of return itself as what makes it uncanny. For Blanchot it would be the alien formality at the heart of the familiar, and indeed at the heart of that most familiar of all things, language, which is uncanny. Familiar: Blanchot's narrators are uncommonly ebullient, light at heart, gay. Uncanny: that gaiety itself is uncanny in Blanchot, mark of the proximity of a radical unconcern with *any* world, concern itself a presence that is put by.

This uncanny familiarity, this grave gaiety is the opposite of Freud's notion of the uncanny as the return of the familiar: it is, to use Blanchot's important observation about Nietzsche, the eternal return ("Je cherchai, cette fois, à l'aborder" begins *Celui qui ne m'accompagnait pas,* a story of endless *reflection,* of thought as *re*-flecting on the interminable, impersonal, unprecedented experience of what happens to thought), but not the eternal return of the same, nor of the already experienced, nor of a world that has been lost but is now resuscitated, simply the pure "appearance of Again, the diva-dame" (Stevens). Freud saw every erotic relation as taking place between at least four people: the lovers and their parents. But in Blanchot true erotic relation is uncountable and takes place without those parents who are for Freud the only ones who count. There is the lover, or narrator, or (usually and by an extreme convention that signifies the intense refusal of the depth of depth psychology) male figure, and an utterly unprecedented other: unprecedented and so beyond the universal precedent of the dialectic of presence and absence.

For Levinas such a relation to the other, to *autrui*, is the hypercategorical imperative to ethics; for Agamben it is the future of the coming community, free to be unprecedented, *qualunque*, uncharacterized and in Blanchot's terms impersonal. For Blanchot, as for Stevens, it is the region haunted by love.

I cite Stevens because I myself wish to reflect on the possibility of an American context for Blanchotian thought, the context for which (in the first instance) Wall offers this extraordinary book. *Love* is a very rare word in Stevens as well, but it is, as I say, a word that he applies to Blanchot, in a letter just four months before his death. In general it is a word that he applies not to people but to places ("Life is an affair of people, not of places. But for me life has been an affair of places, and that has made all the difference"), as in "Notes Towards a Supreme Fiction," where

The Captain loved the ever-hill Catawba,
And therefore married Bawda whom he found there,
And Bawda loved the captain as she loved the sun.

They married well because the marriage-place
Was what they loved. It was neither heaven nor hell.
They were love's characters come face to face.

Their love is an affair of places, but the marriage place, the place they love, or the place they *live* and that Stevens loves is literary space: "From this the poem springs, that we live in a place / That is not our own, and much more, not ourselves, / And hard it is in spite of blazoned days." In the prefatory verse to "Notes" Stevens asks,

> And for what, except for you, do I feel love?
> Do I press the extremest book of the wisest man
> Close to me, hidden in me day and night?
> In the uncertain light of single, certain truth,
> Equal in living changingness to the light
> In which I meet you, in which we sit at rest
> For a moment, in the central of our being,
> The vivid transparence that you bring is peace.

Whom is this addressed to? What is the light in which they meet—the light not of truth, but another light with another clarity? ("Robins and doves are both early risers and are connoisseurs of daylight before the actual presence of the sun coarsens it" says Stevens in a letter.) These lines are a *tutoiement,* and it's not that we cannot know whom they're addressed to, it's that there is no knowing, the addressee does not belong to the world of knowledge. The scholar writes the book, Stevens will say, hot for an accessible bliss, but the bliss the work offers can never be accessible, can never be present.

It is the literary work that gives us the most ineluctable model of what it is that there is no knowing. You can love a work, but you can never know it, even if you love it, especially if you love it, and this is a lesson not about the work (about which there is no learning) but about love.

For Freud to love the literary work (since it is the work that Stevens addresses his dedication to) is to be engaged in transferential fantasy, to love what aids such fantasy. But for Levinas, Blanchot, and Agamben, as for Proust and Stevens before them, love of another can only be intimated through the strange and elusive and always lost love of literature. Stevens: "In poetry you must love the words, the ideas and images and rhythms with all your capacity to love anything at all." The relation to the other that love names, and that Blanchot explores in all his fiction, culminating in *L'attente l'oubli,* is one of radical passivity, interminable attention, the most formal and demanding maintenance of the severest familiarity. Love's characters are, make up, literature. It is only in this strange language, the other language, the language of literature, that love can be uttered (as the parable about the narrator's addressing Claudia in her native language in *L'Arrêt de mort* also makes clear).

This love is what Wall utters in this remarkable book. He too knows what it is to translate the untranslatable and he has found a gravity of style answering the gravity of the otherness of the language he attends to. He will, I imagine, defamiliarize—or (what is the same thing) render uncannily familiar—these works for French and Italian speakers who will find the transmutation Blanchot speaks of: he will render their language plural as he renders English plural, able at last to translate these figures in answerable style, preserving all their alterity and giving back to English, as Stevens also had done, a sense of its own alterity, a place from which the poem may continue to spring.

WILLIAM FLESCH
BRANDEIS UNIVERSITY

Acknowledgments

The author wishes to express his gratitude to a number of friends whom he enlisted for much-needed help. The following people have left their marks on this book: Susie Brubaker, Stephen Duca, Stephen Wall, Magenta Widner, Kate Gardner, Karl Dudick, and the staff of the legendary *Left Bank Books* in Seattle, Washington.

The author would also like to thank Douglas Brick, Camillo Penna, Robert Thomas, Jean-Luc Nancy, and Giorgio Agamben, who read the manuscript and offered critical and encouraging comments.

With affection and respect, the author wishes to acknowledge his teachers. Among them are Mike Wing, Jane Green, Randy Fezel, Charlie Altieri, Carl Dennis, and Evan Watkins.

Introduction

Passivity

The writers we will examine here share a certain preoccupation with a point of radical passivity that affects subjectivity prior to any memory. Passive with regard to the image (Maurice Blanchot), the Other (Emmanuel Levinas), and being-in-language (Giorgio Agamben), each writer cannot resist turning round and round the paradox—or the inverted essence—of this passivity. Namely: passivity in the radical sense, before it is simply opposed to activity, is passive with regard to *itself*, and thus it submits to itself as though it were an exterior power. Hence, radical passivity conceals, or harbors in itself, or communicates with, a *potentia*; it is always outside itself and is its own other. Passive with regard to itself, the essential passivity of the subject must undergo itself, suffer itself, feel itself *as other*. In this sense, passivity is purely passionate.

Older than any (actual) possibility is this *potentia-in-general* that "gives" nothing (except itself) and that "is given" prior to any real state of affairs. Always older than any activity, this radical passivity "gives" its own withdrawal, therefore. It is *and is not* the subject. More intimate than any perception, experience, or feeling, radical passivity "gives" nonpresence, inequality-in-itselfness: i.e., *the incalculable specificity of destruction.* This paradox would remain a merely frustrating formality were it not for the fact that *existence* is the name for this passivity that suffers itself outside itself. Prior to any given being, in short, is the existence that destroys itself as a presence with a destruction that leaves everything intact. It is a very destructive destruction—one that cannot conserve itself in order to destroy; one that cannot but incessantly destroy itself. If you like, this paradox describes the "production" of nothing, or the "production" of an absolute past or an extreme youth that the subject *never has been.* That is to say, radical passivity produces the imaginary, produces something like fiction, something that remains only *possibly* intelligible.

    We have learned from Heidegger that existence is *possibility in general* and therefore it is unrealizable in particular, or it is impossible in particular. Existence as the generality of the possible is precisely the impossible: the uncanny impossibility of *Da-sein*—the being I myself am at my ownmost. That is to say, before I take on the particularity of a person, I am— and am not—an extreme possibility. To say it even better, I am a *potential* possibility: the null event of an inactuality. But what *exposes* this *potentia* I am at my ownmost? What exposes *Da-sein?*

    Blanchot, Levinas, and Agamben provide answers, each of which says the same thing: When there is nothing (when there is fascination with the image, when the other is rendered anonymous and becomes Other, when language itself speaks), the experience of this nothing destroys itself as an experience and exposes a passivity that in fact commands a return to the inexhaustible, uncontrollable, and uncanny *passion* I *must be.* When there is nothing, we are trying to say, there is already no longer nothing. Nihilism is not the final resting place for human being. With nihilism's global completion in the form of the spectacle, Agamben argues specifically, there is still something to be destroyed with a nonconservative destruction that will alter everything while changing not a thing. If you like, we (but this "we" does not name us—it is the not-yet who we still must be) must destroy in a radical movement that leaves nothing to be restored, nothing to be redeemed. We must seize destruction as obsessively as passivity destroys, by failing to complete the work of destruction.

Each of the writers we shall discuss in what follows returns obsessively to the paradox we have described (somewhat too rapidly, no doubt) as radical passivity. They have radicalized their particular disciplines to the point where we can no longer associate what they say with anything like what would commonly fall under the headings "ethics," "aesthetics," or "politics." For each, these categories are always already the trace of a *general* or a *potential* relation that any particular discipline only restricts. Thus each speaks a language at once familiar and alienating. *Each says very little*, if we mean by this that each fails to produce a corpus of thought we may debate amongst ourselves. There are no pros and cons with regard to the works we shall discuss. There will have been, however, the repeated exposure to impossibility that we may take to be an irreducible experience of an intimacy empty of itself, and as fragile as it is repetitive.

In our first chapter we will follow Levinas's analysis of the artwork as that whose (enigmatic) being is precisely its inertia, or its inability to enter the robust present. We will then argue that the weakness or impotence "exhibited" in the artwork opens, not a world, but a *general* ethics and politics.

The artwork "lets go" of the object and thus interrupts the work of subjectivity. The work of art is purely and simply an image, and an image eludes all attempts to grasp it.

In our second chapter, we will argue that Levinas's ethics is imaginary. That is, like an image, *Autrui* will always have remained unavailable to any present and, like a fissure in being, will provoke an infinite rapport that will overwhelm the subject in a flood of responsibility. (This responsibility, however, like jealousy in Proust, will no longer resemble what is commonly meant by the term.) Levinas would probably disagree with our reading since we will claim that that which incessantly escapes—*Autrui*—is an alterity that the *moi* itself is. We will argue that the germ of Levinas's *Autrement qu'être ou au-delà de l'essence*—substitution—is a radical identification of the self with the Other that evacuates the self of sameness, stability, and self-certainty. In becoming responsible for-the-Other, the self encounters an incessance that resembles Blanchotian dying and Agamben's capacity to "not not-be." It *becomes an image*, in short, but no longer an image of itself. It becomes an image of nothing, of no one. It becomes the anonymity that, in fact, *Autrui* already is. Hence the paradox of an identification with no one that is the thesis of our second chapter.

In our third chapter, we examine Blanchot's notion of an imaginary that precedes the real, precedes the object. In particular, we will be attentive to an imaginary language or an incessant murmur that must be silenced in order for the word to "work." This murmur is poetic language: language that has become an image of language, an image of negation. "Older" than the Hegelian negative is a simulated language that poetry cannot but speak. That which poetry each time says will be nothing more than the empty totality of language itself. Before anything is communicated, communication itself is communicated. When someone gestures to me, for example, how do I know that there is an attempt to communicate even if the person speaks a foreign tongue? A mute communication precedes any *dit* (said). This communication is unspoken but irreducible. It is an image of communication that precedes any message. Language that precedes itself, or that "begins" in repetition, is poetry, and this preemptive "speaking" belongs to no subjective intention to say anything. Older than the subject, it is a language spoken by no one, or by an anonymous "someone" (Blanchot's *il*, "he," the Neuter), who cannot speak in the first person. Unable not to communicate, this anonymity cannot cease "his" saying just as it is unable to manifest "himself" in any statement, for "he" *is* only insofar as, and for as long as, "he" speaks. Coinciding so perfectly with "himself," "he" just as perfectly escapes "himself" or is outside "himself." "He" (or "Someone," for it is always another) is perfectly *in* language. Unable to turn around and grasp himself in a reflection without losing himself again, this "Someone's" only being is that repetitive Levinasian *dire* (saying) that unsays itself. It is our thesis in this chapter that the Blanchotian writer is the one who is "capable" of this inability to cease to speak. Refusing all self-presence, this anonymity nevertheless is a hollowing out that makes possible all presence, all work, and all thinking. "Someone," in short, is language itself. "Someone's" being is so utterly absorbed in language without any residue that there is no longer anyone left to save or manifest.

In this way, through Blanchot, we come to Agamben's notion of a community-to-come that is already "in" language and that is no longer graspable as sacrificed, recognized, and identified. Central to Agamben's recent work is the notion of complete being-in-language without any residue. We believe therefore that his work unfolds from Blanchot's *la communauté inavouable,* although Agamben seems to want to deny this. In Agamben's terms, the Blanchotian writer would be someone who cannot not speak and who has become capable of this impotence (like a literary Glenn Gould, to use Agamben's own example). Blanchot (or "Blanchot") is completely absorbed in language, is an image of himself, but as he is completely absorbed in language, he is outside himself and is thus an image of no one. "Blanchot" is the name of an infinite dispersion: language itself as a pure *potentia,* or as the emptiness or pure exteriority that is not a "beyond" but instead an eternal return to a never-having-been or an extreme youth. Agamben suggests that our era—the era of the image, of the spectacle, of the evacuation of all beliefs and presuppositions, indeed, of the Real itself—offers us this return to a never-having-been as an eternal last hope. The essence of the Spectacle (like the logic of the image we examine in our first chapter) is to subtract or even insist on the absence of the object, and thus immediately to depart from simple representation. To be sure, we can still seek in the image for that of which we are cheated (as many of my students often try to find in professional wrestling some of the reality of Greco-Roman wrestling so that they can make of Hulk Hogan the degraded image of an Olympic champion), but we can also *cease* to do this. We can let the prestige of that which is represented (the model) dissolve *in* the image.

Any commentary on the writings of Levinas, Blanchot, and Agamben will be difficult, because each writes in such a way that our power to read is neutralized and dispersed. Each of these thinkers writes in such a way that communication is interrupted, and any formal presentation of their thought, such as ours here, is ceaselessly postponed. To put it most bluntly, they repeat themselves endlessly. (This is particularly true of Levinas and Blanchot, who repeat *each other* as well as echo themselves.) For each of them, striving to say the unsayable, writing is a communication that interrupts itself and comes back to itself in a suspension that will precede nothing and thus refuse the present. The notion of radical suspension is not merely a theoretical nicety. It is the very *un*power of the language of poetry. Radical suspension opens us to a hollow interval of nonsalvageable time that is both without continuation and also without cessation. It will have been a time that departs from the robust time of geometric chronology.

We bring together and overlap three thinkers here to the extent that each articulates an extreme passivity, expropriation, de-nucleation, or neutrality that is paradoxically *constitutive* of the self, the image, or the community. To be sure, other thinkers have devoted themselves to various versions of radical passivity. Georges Bataille, Gilles Deleuze, Luce Irigaray, Philippe Lacoue-Labarthe, and Jean-Luc Nancy are among those who have fashioned their own versions of the enigma. Beyond these more recent thinkers there are, of course, Heidegger's thinking of finitude, Nietzsche's thought of the Eternal Return, and even, in a certain sense, Kant's conception of the Transcendental Imagination (as we shall examine in our chapter on Agamben). No doubt we are forgetting still others, but this only attests to the fact that there can be no historicizing of what is precisely a point of dispersion: the singularity of an enigma that "saves" multiplicity such that even the term "enigma" (which we borrow from Levinas) must be submitted to its displacement in a series of other terms such as *dissemination, désistance, différance, point d'autrui,* and still others that are as well known. Hence the restlessness, imposition, superimposition, disparity, contestation, conflict, and obliqueness that (de)constitutes this population of thinkers. "Philosophy is philosophers in an intersubjective 'intrigue' that nobody resolves, while nobody is allowed a lapse of attention or a lack of rigor,"[1] Levinas tells us. In this sense, each of these thinker's discourses is an "each time" of the enigma itself since the enigma of de-nucleation is the very taking-place of communicativity itself, as we want to show. Always the "same" enigma, communicativity *is* only as trace or iteration without identity. This population of thinkers then, from which we have plucked three, is a community without commonality, without substance or essence.

If we focus on these three thinkers in particular, it is not to focus on any particular ethics, literature, or politics, but instead to approach that which in each text touches on any ethics, literature, or politics whatever, and which each writer exposes in diverse ways. We could, perhaps, have written exclusively on Heidegger, or Heidegger with Kant (of the *Kantbuch*), or Nietzsche (with and against Heidegger), since this population (more or less) schematizes the abyss we today inherit and experience constantly in our thinking. Instead, we confine ourselves to thinkers who confine themselves to problems traditionally "secondary" to fundamental philosophy (even if, in fact, Levinas wishes to institute ethics as "first philosophy"). In each case, these "secondary" concerns become very strange, unfamiliar, not to say *imaginary* (i.e., properly belonging to no category at all). Each thinker we examine here is a strange specialist whose attention to ethical, literary, and political problems has led him into an obscure relation with language itself and mutatis mutandis with time. Each opens his discipline onto a dimension in which language becomes imaginary (anonymous, spoken by no one), and in which time diverges from the State-time of chronological progress, increase, and improvement to which capitalist modernity compulsively sacrifices itself. To put it succinctly: We are modern to the extent that we are sick with continuous, fleeting, and geometric time, and we are Other to the extent that we are—in a nutshell—finite. But the experience of finitude, of *primordial* temporality, is, as we know from Heidegger, rigorously unreachable. We are *precisely* not equal to it. It is the passion of the Outside, as Blanchot might say. But the Outside is not the Beyond and so, simplifying things, we will say that we are interested in Levinas to the extent that he *fails* to reveal or institute an ethical Beyond; we are interested in Blanchot to the extent that he involves us in this incessant limiting that is the very passion of the (not) Beyond *(le pas au-delà);* and we are interested in Agamben insofar as he makes of this ambiguous limit an inescapable and unexcludable "belonging." More narrowly, we are interested in a Blanchotian "elemental depth" that precedes access to any accomplishment. That is to say, we are interested in an anteriority that informs the Levinasian *éthique,* the Blanchotian *littéraire,* and the Agambenian *Quodlibet ens.*

Beginning with Levinas's 1948 essay "Réalité et son ombre," we proceed to show how aspects of that analysis inform both his own notion of a rapport with the Other that precedes egology, and also informs Blanchot's notions of writing and the imaginary. We then will read Blanchot's *L'arrêt de mort* as a work "structured" by nonaccomplishment and struggle (or, if you will, "structured" by finitude). From there we analyze Agamben's *La comunità che viene* in light of Heidegger's reading of Kantian schematism in order to show an affinity between it and the Blanchotian imaginary that, in the end, we claim is the very "place" of communicativity and its radical passivity.

We are arguing that the point to which each thinker we examine leads us is the point of communicativity *as such,* insofar as this point is in itself an interruption of communication. That is to say, communicativity *pulverizes* discourse. It gives nothing to be thought; it gives no message to which we might listen but, in effect, says: there is *(il y a).* Communicativity *as such*—where *what* is communicated is not outside it but instead buries language in itself—is poetry, the original and absolute singularity of what does not cease to take place. *Communication*, then, is the pure form of the separation of communicativity from itself, or, in a word, (chronological) time. Poetry, however, is an experience of time that is radically discontinuous. It is the time of futurity that does not lie in a future either remote or just around the corner, but rather in the infinitive "to" of the "to come" (or *à venir*) to which we shall refer numerous times throughout this book. In poetry, that which speaks is the very "to" of "to speak." Poetry says the pure *there*, or the pure possibility of any relation whatever, and it is only to the pure *there* that we ("properly," finitely) belong; but we belong such that no residue remains upon which we may reflect, no residue or pleat that would allow us the ability to grasp and auto-originate ourselves. Empty of itself, or different in itself, we "originate," thus, in the incessant repetition of the *there*. This will be the "original experience" of which Blanchot speaks in *L'espace littéraire*.

The Language of Poetry

Merveilleuse hypocrite! Car elle aime la folie qu'elle surveille.

—Levinas

Poetry is language that makes itself felt like the bodies of liars and impostors that brush up against us daily on the street. According to Levinas, the language of poetry does not "name a species whose genus is referred to by the word art."[2] If Paul Celan "sees no difference between a poem and a handshake,"[3] it is because poetry, refractory to the categories of thought, is thingish, like another body, or like the words we speak at a funeral. Those dying words weigh like things in our mouths because they are no longer able to refer to anything real. The language of poetry is the very weakness of meaning that remains when the real is withdrawn from our powers. This funereal language weighs in my mouth as a thing and is offered to others as a useless gift because it can no longer disappear into the labor of referring. In the lugubrious atmosphere of the funeral, words are that which maintain contact with a profoundly paralyzed time. No longer able to refer, language is imperceptibly transformed because it begins to resemble itself. Unable to reveal or aver, words are lost between meaning and showing, between saying and seeing, and they depart from the straightforwardness of intentionality as if lured by another destiny. Insofar as I cannot separate myself from these words that linger on my tongue—words that are no longer my own since they have defected from my meaning-to-say—they involve me in that other destiny of which they are already a part.

Recently, in a television newscast, we saw the story of an elderly woman whose husband had passed away on the floor of their home. She placed a blanket over the body and he remained there, as if under the blanket, for a number of years until a social worker discovered the "bizarre" situation. The woman had continued to live, in the meantime, more or less as she had before, as best she could, given the solitude and failing strength of advanced age. Apparently, she never denied to herself that her husband was dead (as did the duchess of Marlboro, who had a statue made of her late husband William Congreve, and seated it at the dinner table, where she would converse with it as if the great dramatist had somehow survived his own death). The social worker who commented on the situation he had discovered said, poignantly, that there was obviously great affection here. Of the most demanding kind, we must add. For hers is not a disturbing love. It is not Isolde's or Salome's love. Hers, we must imagine, is a most irreparable, profane, and absolutely impoverished love (to borrow some terms from Agamben that seem to belong in this context): love for her husband, for the unredeemed, unburied, overly present body her husband was, and was not. She did not, it seems, long for the withdrawn being her husband had been, but instead remained faithful to the death her husband could not accomplish. This could only have led her astray in her madness (if we must call it that), scattering her affection everywhere in the house because her husband could no longer occupy his proper place. We imagine that she must have enjoyed an elemental intimacy, profound and without qualifications.

The peculiar intimacy and intensity that traditionally belong to literature are a fidelity to ambiguity that scatters intimacy everywhere, multiplying it to infinity, like the snowflakes that fell down upon Brekhounov as he lay down upon Nikita, in the tale from Tolstoy of which Blanchot is so fond.[4] In this study we would like to say very little. We would prefer to be like the elderly woman who did very little for her husband upon his demise. She merely placed a blanket over him. We would merely want to note that in the image, in the narrative, in the other person—as it were, "in parenthesis" (or in quotation marks) or, if you prefer, *under erasure* (because the parentheses are invisible and cannot be admitted into the narrative proper, yet introduce into the story an element that is felt without being acknowledged, like an aphonic voice that says "keep me in mind but do not think about me")—one enters a maze of rumor and innuendo as if one's power to read, to see, and to tell had become defective, aorist, metamorphosed, and supererogatory.

ONE

The Allegory of Being

Image

Levinas begins his 1948 essay on art, "La réalité et son ombre," simply enough. As everyone knows, the artist substitutes an image for a concept. Uninterested in the intelligibility of the object, the artist does not maintain a real relationship with the object by knowing it, grasping it, and putting it to work. By substituting an image for the concept, all real relations with the object are neutralized. Artistic "disinterest" is just this blindness to concepts, Levinas says. The artistic gaze neutralizes vision and perception. It is not an act. It is a nonconcerning, nonknowing gaze. It does not cross a distance in order to grasp an object as does the hand that labors or the consciousness that seizes the thing in an act of recognition. The simple, elementary substitution of the image for the concept inverts all directionality, all conscious "aiming-at." The image that the artist substitutes for the concept is not another object and does not behave like an object. In everyday life, in everyday commerce with things, the seized object tends to disappear into its usefulness, its function, its familiarity. Art arrests this movement of recognition and industry. In art, that which vanishes into utility and knowledge reappears outside its usefulness, outside all real relations, in a space strictly uncrossable, infinitely fragile, only proximally *there* at all, as if its existence had been paralyzed, or as if the object led a phantom existence parallel to its truth.

The image is fundamentally or essentially passive. It eludes all attempts to seize it because it occupies empty space. An image, quite simply, is nothing. Our relation with the image "marks a hold over us rather than our initiative [marque une emprise sur nous, plutôt que notre initiative],"[1] Levinas says. The image contrasts with concepts or, more precisely, it is the very event of contrasting with concepts. Precisely to the extent that I do not act on, know, or think the thing in its concept, there is an inversion of my everyday relationship with the object, and subjectivity is pushed to an extreme pole of passivity. Unable to seize an image, I participate in its imaginary dimension. This passivity can be observed, Levinas points out, in music, dance, and magic.[2] To this list we may add trance, hysterical possession, and hypnotic suggestion. In short, the image inspires and it is just the image that inspires, not the object it represents. *Precisely when there is nothing and just insofar as there is nothing, the image exercises its impotent power.* Rhythm and participation are the "exceptional structure of aesthetic existence [la structure exceptionelle de l'existence esthétique]" and are also the way "the poetic order affects us [l'ordre poétique nous affecte]."[3] This involvement, importantly, is not "beyond" representation. It is, to the contrary, the profound involvement of the subject *in* its own representations. Profound because their "entry into us is one with our entry into them [entrent en nous ou nous entrons en eux, peu importe]," and therefore "in this rhythm there is no longer a oneself but a sort of passage from oneself to anonymity [dans le rythme il n'y a plus de *soi*, mais comme un passage de soi à l'anonymat]."[4]

The participation itself is an unrepresentable movement. In aesthetic existence there is an indistinction between who is possessed or affected and that which possesses or affects. Levinas notes in passing that this simultaneity of possession and dispossession has a role in ecstatic rites. Aesthetic existence involves us in an indistinction of "same" and "other." It is thus a truly unrepresentable moment (but not a "beyond") wherein the density of being in its "here" is invaded by a "nowhere," a "nothing." Rhythm cannot be objectified; it can only be dramatized, enacted, suffered. It is experienced as indistinction, as myself-as-other. Unable to hang on to its freedom, the subject experiences an exteriority in which it cannot but mistake itself for another. That is, the subject ceases to experience itself *as* itself. Totally absorbed in the scene, consciousness, having nothing to aim at, becomes supererogatory, as does the body, for, at once actor and spectator, the body is transformed into sensations belonging to no one, or belonging to an anonymous Someone whose organs of perception have defected. Hence the fear of the artistic milieu that is attested to in the nervous anxiety so many people feel in the crowded concert hall or the august museum.

An image, Levinas says, is essentially musical insofar as it detaches itself from the object as does sound from that which makes the sound.[5] In the aesthetic experience, this detachment is an essential atmosphere. In fact, however, this atmosphere is everywhere because images are everywhere. Indeed, the whole world wears on its face its own image and we are thus permitted to think a dimension of aesthetic participation that is general and not restricted to the movie theater or concert hall. This general dimension of profound participation would, then, subtend consciousness and industry at every moment. Industrial language necessarily fails to tell of this involvement, for this profound participation defects from "every moment" of subjectivity (i.e., of initiative and power). The deconceptualization of reality that art realizes restrictedly is, in fact, a generalized impersonality that lies "below" all knowing. If you like, an ecstatic rite shadows all cognition. Where being-in-the-world involves existence in concepts and truth, ecstatic sensations depart from each moment of being-in-the-world and involve us in a disincarnation of the real simply because of the image (the nonobject, or the music) that is on the face of all that is in the world. Beneath or beside one's conceptual commerce with the world there remains a rhythmic participation whose immediacy drives out all thought. Aesthetic existence, in short, is perpetually suggestive, affirmative, influential, impersonal, and immemorial. It is as if in the real itself a band of Sirens had always called to us, as in Blanchot's retelling of the fabulous episode from Homer.[6]

Art realizes the paradox of immediacy—the paradox of an immediacy that drives out all mediation and, essentially empty, drives out itself and is thus outside memory. Disincarnate and impersonal, aesthetic existence cannot enter into any present (or it "dies" when forced to, as do the Sirens in Blanchot's essay). It is thus intolerable to thought. Not the minutest sliver of reflection or temporal lag makes room for subjective initiative or action. The music lover no doubt feels great passion as she listens to a beloved piece, but it is not certain that she feels *herself* in the passion. Paradoxically, immediacy unhinges me from myself. The proximity of art to magic and trance indicates a trajectory wherein the subject experiences a fainting away of self altogether, and an exposure to exteriority. The body has a membrane, a skin, but the self does not. The "magical" conversion of the object into an image, a nonobject, a nothing, triggers the immediacy of passionate involvement. While retaining the form, colors, sound, and other qualities of the object, the image, in effect, "drives the object out of the world [chasser les objets du monde]" and thus "breaks up representation [briser la représentation]"[7] because the image subtracts the object to be represented from the representation. The image disincarnates the real, but this is so only because the real is always already approached by its image: "The whole of our world, with its elementary and intellectually elaborated givens, can touch us musically, can become an image [L'ensemble de notre monde, avec ses données et élémentaires et intellectuellement élaborées, peut nous toucher musicalement, devenir image]."[8] Art in general realizes this latency and perpetually effaces the difference between the real and the imaginary, nature and mimesis. "La réalité et son ombre" is thus an introduction to the important recent work done by Philippe Lacoue-Labarthe on radical, or non-Platonic (i.e., nonrestricted, that is to say, *general*) mimesis.[9]

Duality

A sign directly refers to its object, but an image resembles it.[10] An image resembles an object, but resemblance is not the result of a comparison between two realms: the real and the imaginary. This is a key point for Levinas in this essay. Audiences who respond to a film by immediately comparing it to some reality often respond energetically and aggressively as if they were being cheated of reality and only the proper comparison could restore the real to itself and keep the two realms separate. In jeopardy is the proper difference between them. But resemblance is not the end result of a comparison. It is that which engenders the image in the first place. Resemblance begins in the real itself:

Here is a person who is what he is; but he does not make us forget, does not absorb, cover over entirely the objects he holds and the way he holds them, his gestures, limbs, gaze, thought, skin, which escape from under the identity of his substance, which like a torn sack is unable to contain them. [. . .] There is then a duality in this person, this thing, a duality in its being. It is what it is and it is a stranger to itself, and there is a relationship between these two moments. We will say the thing is itself and is its image. And that this relationship between the thing and its image is resemblance.

[Voici une personne qui est ce qu'elle est; mais elle ne fait pas oublier, n'absorbe pas, ne recouvre pas entièrement les objets qu'elle tient et la manière dont elle les tient, ses gestes, ses membres, son regard, sa pensée, sa peau, qui s'échappent de sous l'identité de sa substance, incapable, comme un sac troué, de les contenir. [. . .] Il y a donc cette personne, dans cette chose une dualité, une dualité dans son être. Elle est ce qu'elle est et elle est étrangère à elle-même et il y a un rapport entre ces deux moments. Nous dirons que la chose est elle-même et son image. Et que ce rapport entre la chose et son image est la ressemblance.][11]

A person or a thing resembles itself and the resemblance is already its "other" destiny: toward the image. This movement of resemblance is obscure. One cannot imagine a thing resembling itself. One simply imagines the thing, of course. This attests to the simultaneity of its being and its appearing. That which appears, however, is detachable from the thing and can end outside the thing on a videotape or in a museum. That a thing is imaginable, that it is sensible, gives it another destiny apart from its truth (from its identity). It is as if that which is imaginable were always already left behind by the thing. Insofar as a thing resembles itself, it departs from itself and can be quoted, or placed in parenthesis, in an image. An image captures and immobilizes this (invisible, unimaginable) movement of a thing-resembling-itself. Art captures that which truth sheds, leaves abandoned, leaks. Art, Levinas tells us summarily, "lets go of the prey for the shadow [l'art lâche donc la proie pour l'ombre]."[12] We are nonetheless entitled to ask: What was the prey? What was lost?

The answer to this question is ambiguous. There is, Levinas says, a duality in being, a nontruth or a defection from truth that is simultaneous with truth. Simultaneous with *being* itself, a thing resembles itself, or flees itself. Giorgio Agamben understands this to mean that a thing is simultaneously itself *and* its qualities without being the same thing as its qualities.[13] A thing, Agamben says, is not its qualities, is not identical to its qualities, but at the same time it is nothing other than its qualities. We shall return to this delicate point in our chapter on Agamben. (Let us note for now, however, that Blanchot reads the same ambiguity through the uncanniness of the cadaver.[14] He points out that the dear departed is nothing other than the cadaver that lies in state. Yet the departed is certainly not the same thing as the corpse, is not identical with the cadaver. The dear departed one is gone, precisely. Yet, in the corpse, the departed comes to resemble herself, or even, *returns* to herself *as* her resemblance, while at the same time absenting herself. There is a sort of erosion at work here that is strictly speaking unthinkable. It is not a case of qualities clinging to some substance, sub-base, or fundament. It is rather the case that resemblance moves to replace the real, that identity seems to be "constituted" by resemblance or qualities without *being* those qualities or that resemblance.)

Levinas finds, therefore, that that which is strange, obscure (but in no way ineffable), and lends itself to art and to myth is this: Being-such-as-it-is, the real in its truth, is already offered to, or is *in*, the imaginary. The being-in-the-imaginary of the real is a kind of originary exoticism. It is the structure of the sensible as such. The sensible character of the thing, its qualities (red, hard, sonorous, aromatic), make it imaginable, and the truth of the thing is nothing other than its being imaginable as such. The real, being, truth, is the place where the imaginary takes place. That which is "lost," the "prey" that art "lets go of" is, quite simply, the very event of the imaginary—an event that cannot be imagined, an event the real is already involved in. (By the way, this is the torment of the Blanchotian writer: he loses the most desired moment, the event of poetic language itself. He is tormented by the presence/absence *in* the image of that which is unimaginable. In short, the real as-it-is is always already becoming an image, an untruth.)

Being is dual. It is simultaneous with itself. Irreducibly ambiguous, it is withdrawn from itself in its very sensibility. Nontruth is the sensible character of the thing. Insofar as a being resembles itself it is sensible, but its sensibility is an obscure essence or fugitivity that "disincarnates" being. I see a thing *as* its image, not *through* it. (Thus, Levinas says that the image is the allegory of being, a point to which we shall return shortly.) The disincarnation of being is the very intensity and essential strangeness of art. But art has its own aggressivity as well. In art, the sensible does not merely depart from the real. It "insists" on the absence of the object. Splashes of color, sound, and bits of foreign matter "occupy [the object's] place fully to mark its removal, as though the represented object died, were degraded, were disincarnated in its own reflection [occupent entièrement sa place pour marquer son éloignement, comme si l'objet représenté mourait, se dégradait, se désincarnait dans son propre reflet]."[15] The massive presence of a corpse wrings so many tears from us because it occupies fully and with excessive completeness the place of the departed loved one. The real is itself *and* it escapes itself. Art does not merely reflect this evasion; it brings it out and completes it. It intensifies it by completing it, by quoting it, by substituting for the truth of the thing its image—as if it was indifferent to the reality of the thing, or as if the reality of the thing counted for nothing. Art places in parenthesis the fugitivity of the real, its ambiguity, and circumscribes a "dimension of evasion [une dimension d'évasion]."[16] Insofar as it does this, it introduces into the world the atmosphere of that temporal interval Levinas calls *l'entretemps*.

To sum up: Insofar as a being resembles itself (apart from *being* itself, that is, apart from the truth proper to its being, i.e., its presence) it is sensible and this sensibility is its nontruth, its shadow. The image does not precede the resembling. The neutralization of space in the image *is* the resemblance that "engenders the image [engendre l'image]."[17] A thing can participate in its truth or in its being, but parallel to this a thing departs from itself in an emission that is phantasmic and is not identical with truth. The quasi existence of this phantasm is a "semblance of existing [semblant d'exister]" or a nontruth without being.[18] (In the chapter on Giorgio Agamben, we shall show that the Italian philosopher makes of this phantasm a pure return to being, but to being purely profaned, that is, stripped of all ineffability and identity.)

The Obscure Temporality of the Artwork

We have seen that an image is musical, that it is rhythmic, but in the last analysis, it is plastic, a statue, a "stoppage of time, or rather its delay behind itself [un arrêt du temps ou plutôt son retard sur lui-même]."[19] The time that seems to be introduced into the art of novels, plays, and cinema can in no way "shatter the fixity of the image [n'ébranle pas la fixité de l'image]."[20] Just as Mona Lisa's smile will never broaden, so will Hamlet eternally agree to meet with the ghost that says it is his father's, and so eternally will Kane suffer the loss of his family, his political ambitions, his empire, and his marriages. The work of art will forever be arrested in the task of accomplishing the work of being. It will forever defect from the time proper to being. Celluloid and paper will of course decay, but *as an image* the artwork will be forever fixed *en l'entretemps*, and this fatality is the central concern of Levinas's essay on art.

Art is an instant that "endures without a future [dure sans avenir]"[21] and even without a duration. For art is an image and an image is, if we may say this, *rigorously* uncertain. It does not even occupy space. An image is an "impersonal and anonymous *instant* [*instant* impersonnel et anonyme]."[22] There is thus something deadly in the puppetry that is art. Unable to force itself into the present and assume a future, art is the intrusion of death into the familiar world. The temporality art realizes, Levinas says, is the temporality of nightmare. Like the *il y a*, the instant of fixity that is the event of art strips freedom of its power to assume the present moment. Art is not the replica of a time that has been suspended halfway through its continuation and abandoned as half-completed like a bridge that stops in midspan. As Levinas has been showing us, art is that which, in the general economy of being, defects from the present. It is that part of being that incessantly moves to its *en deçà*, its "interstice," as if each moment of (chronological) time were simultaneously a moment of fate. This should remind us of a point that is important to Levinas's work as a whole. He conceives of time as a series of instants sutured together but infinitely fragile, always shadowed by the possibility of congealing into an image and thus of withdrawing from our powers.[23]

Being is dual. It doubles up and resembles itself, and the temporality of art is carved out of this repetition. It is in this way that the real itself solicits the artist, since it is always already involved in its own shadow and thus is already vulnerable to the temporal modification that is the image, the narrative, the history. An artist is a person who is fascinated by the plasticity of the real. He or she is one who, as Blanchot says, "lives the event as an image [vivre un événement en image],"[24] that is, who experiences the event insofar as it is *already* an image (or already resembles itself and is detached from the real). Levinas puts it this way: "Life solicits the novelist when it seems to him as if it were already something out of a book [La vie sollicite le romancier quand elle lui apparaît comme si elle sortait déjà d'un livre]."[25] This means that there is already something artificial about the real, something aesthetic, uncanny, plastic—if you like, something fake. Life is always very nearly a novel, an image, a corpse. Put differently, the real is always vulnerable to the stoppage of time—to the image of finitude—that it wears on its face. Insofar as this person resembles herself, she is infinitely vulnerable, infinitely fragile, as an image is fragile. A strange weakness pervades her that we cannot grasp, a bleeding we cannot stanch. She is not the same thing as her resemblance to herself, but she is nothing other than it. Human reality is nothing other than this infinite vulnerability, inequality-in-itself, or difference-in-itself. It is as if the face of things were another body, a body "made up of" fragility and that takes the place of personal presence. We may wish to say that this is an infinite vulnerability to death. However, the ontological signification is doubled by the fugitivity of the image: a derelict time unable to become present and that insists on the absence of being, but as if absence itself had been immobilized in its approach and could not even achieve the absence the image so dramatically insists on.

Levinas goes on to say in this essay that art is "the uncertainty of [time's] continuation [l'incertitude de sa continuation],"[26] the possibility that time can stop. This anxiety attests to a dimension of time that peels itself away from chronology as though "a whole set of facts was already immobilized and formed a series [comme si toute une suite de faits s'immobilisaient et formaient série]."[27] The real, at its surfaces, on its face, offers itself to art as if it was already plastic. The artist participates solely in the shadow dimension. The very intimacy and intensity of art are its attentiveness to what appears, to what is at the surface, to that which incessantly comes to the surface—resemblance. It is at her surfaces that a person is nearly petrified, nearly captured (but it is here that she is also essentially fugitive, for the image flees the present). This incessant coming to the surface is the obscurity of the time of dying, as Levinas proceeds to make clear. The time of dying is not the cross section of a continuum. Instead, "The time of *dying* itself cannot give itself the other shore. What is unique and poignant in this instant is due to the fact that it cannot pass. In *dying*, the horizon of the future is given, but the future as promise of a new present is refused; one is in the interval, forever an interval [Le temps-même du *mourir* ne peut pas se donner l'autre rive. Ce que cet instant a d'unique et de poignant tient au fait de ne pas pouvoir passer. Dans le *mourir*, l'horizon de l'avenir est donnée, mais, l'avenir en tant que promesse du présent nouveau est refusé—on est dans l'intervalle, à jamais intervalle.]."[28] This *dying*, Levinas says, "is the great obsession of the artist's world [la grande obsession du monde artiste]."[29] An instant of time may not have another shore. It may be sutured into time's *l'entretemps*, outside any continuum, and stop just short of the present. It is as if living time were simultaneously sutured into a plastic series, a ceaseless interval departing from any continuity. Or it is as if being-as-it-is, in its truth, were also irreparably consigned to nontruth, to immobilization in the image—buried alive, as in Poe. Art realizes the possibility that living being can always be experienced as an image, as unliving, as always already petrified—as if qualities clung to nothing at all.

The Space of Art

Art is then something horrible, "something inhuman and monstrous [quelque chose d'inhumain et de monstrueux]"[30] because it is powerless, because it cannot go beyond, because it cannot even end. Art is radical passivity. It "shows" this passivity in the stoppage of time *en deçà du temps*. Its value to civilization is ambiguous since it is utterly foreign to the world of initiative. It shows the world the obscurity of fate not as an elsewhere that comes from beyond to intervene in the present, but as the very face the world wears. Art accomplishes this feat by way of irresponsibility. Outside all labor, art beckons to us as if all life could end up in myth, in plasticity, in the "rhythm of a reality which solicits only its admission into a book or a painting [le rhythme d'une réalité qui ne sollicite que son admission dans un livre ou dans un tableau]."[31] It is as if art could replace the building up of a habitat, a world, the establishment of justice, governments, the city itself. Ultimately "horrible," art nonetheless beckons to us in the same way that a rhythm is irresistibly engaging.

Levinas concludes, therefore, that art, aesthetic existence, rhythm, simultaneous possession and dispossession, and irresponsibility are a part of life and have a place, "but only a place, in human happiness [mais une place seulement—dans le bonheur de l'homme]."[32] Criticism, insofar as it approaches the artistic event as such, reintroduces the inhumanity of art back into the world. As we have seen, this will not involve a comparison of the artwork to some reality. It involves treating the artwork as a myth: "[T]his immobile statue has to be put in movement and made to speak [cette statue immobile, il faut la mettre en mouvement et la faire parler]."[33] It involves, in short, interrupting myth and integrating that which is excessively closed to language back into the language from which it defected.[34] Myth is the source of philosophical truth, for it is, as the moment of resemblance, the distance the real takes from itself—its ambiguity and duality. Art is an inversion of creation.[35] It presents to the world the vulnerability of congealing into an image that all creation is prey to, and philosophy and criticism can ally themselves with creation only by "skipping over the intervals of the meanwhile [en sautant les intervalles de l'entretemps]."[36] In effect, this means that philosophy and criticism can only begin by "forgetting" art.

For, like an idol, Levinas says, an artwork is "stupid."[37] We must add that every artist since Pygmalion has known this. Art is a caricature of life, not another, better, life. The artwork cannot assume or take on life. It overflows life on all sides, like water without a container. Unable to attain the present moment, the artwork spills all the aspirations the artist built into it. Art can only empty itself of all the artist's efforts.

The elementary procedure of art is to substitute an image for a concept. But the artist cannot be said to aim at the image per se as a goal. Art (except in advertising) does not wish to limit itself to an image, however perfect or beautiful. Neither does the artist aim at an elusive essence nor ineffability, as do philosophy and criticism. Art aims to remain in contact with that which is *unmade in its own image [défait selon son im-*

age]," as Blanchot puts it.[38] Art remains in contact with that which is infinitely vulnerable to disincarnation—that which is neither itself in its truth nor in its image (its double, or its other fate). The substitution of the image for the concept is only the first step, for when the image has succeeded in driving the object out of existence, what remains? What is the image when it is no longer an image of . . . ? Neither the thing nor its double, the artwork is at once the trace of no origin. If art "lets go of the prey for the shadow," and if the "insecurity of a being that has a presentiment of its fate is the great obsession of the artist's world," this is because art maintains contact with the imaginary space left empty of all substance and inhabited by no one—the space that being spills out into, beside itself. In this space (Blanchot's *l'espace littéraire*), the real is already imaginary and detached from its truth, its identity. In this space, the plasticity of matter no longer refers to the substance to which qualities cling but to the arrested death that is the rigorous immobility of the statue. It is ambiguous space and it is the most subtle of bodies, for it is neither substance nor image but rather the liquidation of the elemental distance that separates the two. This space belongs neither to art nor to philosophy, neither to the image nor to the concept. In contrast to the philosopher, the artist is allied with the very weakness of space itself: communication or sheer communicativity—the pure "there is" *(il y a)*. (Blanchot, in our opinion, has gone further than any other writer in our times toward making this space "speak.")

"Inert matter," Levinas says, "already refers to a substance to which its qualities cling. In a statue, matter knows the death of idols [La matière inert se réfère déjà une substance à laquelle s'accrochent ses qualités. Dans la statue, la matière connaît la mort de l'idole]."[39] This means that in art matter will encounter the inversion of creation that is *l'entretemps*. In the inversion, apart from the inertia of matter and already withdrawn from the thing-for-us, there is the for-no-one that characterizes the Neuter. Neutral with respect to *what* is, art, which substitutes the image for the concept, "presents" the sheer *that there is*, or anteriority as such. This is the atmosphere of art and this neutralization is unmediated and immediate, and thus eludes all cognition and all memory. The artwork is a thing-for-no-one, and it thus induces from us involvements that do not originate in our initiative. This allows Blanchot to say that "the image is intimate because it makes of our intimacy an exterior power that we submit to passively [intime est l'image parce qu'elle fait de notre intimité une puissance exterieure que nous subissons passivement]."[40] The sheer *that there is*, or the *il y a*, is ungraspable. It eludes every present yet it is that without which there will never have been any possibility as such. Art does not merely present, as Levinas stresses, the possibility that time can stop. It also, more affirmatively, presents *possibility itself* as that which eludes everything—possibility as (the) nothing, as immediate. Which amounts to saying that nothing, or *the* nothing, is the form of any possible relation.

Presented as arrested, the atmosphere of art presents the return of that which can never be excluded but which, at the same time, excludes everything. In the space of literature qualities cling to nothing, to no being. Something eludes cognition, but makes itself felt (if obscurely) as that which is never "itself," that which is only "suggested." Something comes but remains arrested in its "meanwhile." For Blanchot this will be the time of writing. It is uncommon, unclassifiable, and anonymous, like an infinite murmur, as Foucault puts it.[41] It is writing that cannot end itself and is continually outside itself like a thing among things. An enormity without proportion, it is the very scratching sound we hear, from somewhere, when we write these things.

The Profane

For both Levinas and Blanchot, the artist neither creates nor reveals. That which the philosopher fixes in the eternity of the concept, art arrests in the interval of the image. Whereas philosophy offers us the thing to know and use, art realizes a withdrawal from power and even, more strongly, a withdrawal from the present. Aesthetic existence is a lapse in our ability to mobilize time. The intimate possibility that time can stop is the possibility of being delivered to a time without us, without a present—impersonal and neutral. This is simulated time, a simulation of existing or an existence outside initiative. It is not the promise of a new beginning and it does not carry us to a *beyond* of being (ethical or otherwise). It only subtracts us from ourselves.

In *La comunità che viene*, Giorgio Agamben will say that the whole of our world has been transformed into an image, a spectacle. This is the starting point for his politics. He will say that the world has come to resemble itself completely, totally, and thus has separated human agency from its traditional initiative. That is to say, the whole of our world can now be experienced as an image and we are no longer able to experience ourselves *in* the world, for its space is now imaginary. Hence, Agamben's interest in the expropriation of experience and his attempts to rescue from this malaise a radical possibility he calls pure being-in-language. His politics is an attempt to appropriate this expropriation (or this impotence outside any initiative) not as another power, but as an unpower that is an ambiguous capacity for irreparability. He will ask that we cease to seek in the imaginary for that which the imaginary suspends—identity—and instead that we rejoin our "oldest" experience: the sheer profanity *that there is*. The sheer *il y a* is without clamor and without pathos. It would be experienced when there is nothing to experience—as in aesthetic existence, precisely. In his analyses of art, Levinas brings out art's "ability" to conserve this experience, and in Blanchot we catch a glimpse into a life outside initiative.

For all three writers, the sheer *that there is* that every image harbors is our separation from any particular experience, but it does not promise a concrete future to which we may relate ourselves. Nevertheless, art remains our manifest orientation towards it. Refusing all grasp, art "says" that time outside the synchrony of the present cannot *but* be lost, that it is nonconsecutive, discontinuous, arresting. If you like, art—the pure form of any possible relation, or anteriority as such—is also the pure form of separation (from the personal and the subjective). That is to say, art is not only the presentiment of fate, it is also *another* death from which we cannot separate ourselves and which we cannot finish, not even in death. It is a loss we cannot let go of, but that does not hold us in it.

For the Levinas of "La réalité et son ombre," the situation of art in the general economy of being is limited because it lacks the perspective of the Other *(Autrui)* that breaks up the spell of art and awakens us to responsibility. But we will want to show, in our next chapter, that the relation with *Autrui* is ambiguous and, if we may say so, imaginary.

TWO

Levinas's Ethics

Today it is art that inherits, before our very eyes, the delirious role and character of the religious. Today it is art that gnaws at and transforms us.
—*Bataille*

Like a Nessus Tunic my skin would be.
—*Levinas*

An Ambiguous Rapport

As if in response to Georges Bataille (whom, to my knowledge, he never cites) Emmanuel Levinas has attempted to define ethics as the privileged site of delirium in our culture. His great book *Autrement qu'être ou au-delà de l'essence* defines the rapport with *Autrui* as the "seed of folly [grain de folie]" in the soul.[1] With increasing complexity and determination he has attempted to articulate a responsibility that realizes in the extreme an abandonment of the certainties and imperialisms of the self. Stranger than art would be the immemorial rapport with the Other. As if to answer Bataille's frequent complaint that, in spite of Kant, we still cannot imagine an ethics that is not "committed," Levinas has described his ethics as "for-the-other *[pour l'autre]*," but "for nothing [pour *rien*];"[2] in short, a sovereign ethics. Ethical obligation would be, for Levinas, uncontainable, and inexorably *betrayed* by morals and laws. It would be, in fact, instability itself: the instability of the naked relation to the Other. For, with Bataille,

31

Levinas takes as his starting point the impossibility of indifference to the Other—to the mortality of the other person—
as the place (or nonplace [non-lieu]) where the self is exposed
and lacerated. His version of Bataille's famous *l'expérience in-
térieur* is *mauvaise conscience:* "the interiority of non-intentional
consciousness [l'intériorité de la conscience non-intentio-
nelle]."³ Insisting, with Bataille, that the demand for an ethics
cannot be subordinated to anything else, all of Levinas's work
aims at a relation to the Other *(Autrui)* "older" than the "relation to the self (egology) and the relation to the world (cos-
mology)."⁴ This olamic relation, he insists, is one of responsibility, and it subtends and interrupts the relation so dispiritingly
described by Freud and others as *homo lupus homini.*

Let us note straightaway, for it will guide our entire reading of Levinas, that as this relation is "older" than the self and
the world, this Other will have always already sunk into immemoriality, prior to any memory or repression. The "relation" then will not involve two terms, the self and the other.
The relation will be "older" than any self. This anteriority
will be, for Levinas, a dissymmetry and a goodness without
measure that (de)structures the self *as* a relation with a never-
present Other. We add, therefore, that any relation that the *I*
establishes with *an* other subject will only betray the pure anteriority that, in Levinas's thought, imperiously *orders* me to the
Other. Furthermore, we must note that, as immemorial, this
anterior relation can *only* be betrayed, and therefore any relation to another remains paradoxically faithful to the Levinasian
éthique. Hence, Levinas offers no critique of any existing ethics or morals, nor does he propose maxims according to which
we must act. All of Levinas's thought gravitates toward this
obsessive relation that refracts all actual relations, holding each
in relation to that immemorial relation which each cannot but
betray. His ethics, in short, is *essentially* ambiguous.

To be sure, this is no ethics that would be recognized as such by Kant or Mill. In a sense, we can say that in fact there is no Levinasian ethics, as it can be said that there is no philosophy of Heidegger, since each is "founded" on an abyss, a "forgetting." Like the relation with Being, the relation with the Other is without an object, an aim, or a purpose. It is a relation that drains consciousness of intentionality, and it is in this relation that Levinas would place the dispossession of self that defines communicativity as such and the opening beyond the confines of any knowing. The relation with the Other (unlike the Heideggerian relation to Being) is not a precomprehension, but a breakup of any comprehension.

We will not be pitting Levinas against Bataille on the question of art (which, as we know, is of limited interest to Levinas) versus ethics. What matters to each of them, in spite of their quite considerable differences, is the singular relation with the other person as that which is the most fragile and the most exposed. It is a relation that withdraws from our powers—a relation too fragile even to qualify as a proper experience. (This relation, in fact, echoes the relation with the image we have discussed elsewhere in this book.) It is impossible, in our opinion, not to be fascinated by Levinas's work, by his relentless focus on a relation that exceeds power and that is only "possible" as impossible, betrayed, or fictioned, because what Levinas runs up against, again and again, with and against Heidegger, is this (as flatly stated by Mikkel Borch-Jacobsen): "There is no ethics, nor morals, of finitude [Il n'y a pas d' 'éthique', pas de 'morale' de la finitude]."[5] What happens in Levinas, what passes under the *word* ethics, is no ethics per se, no relation as such. What happens is a relation that is no relation, that cannot but be betrayed, and by which I cannot but be obligated, because the "essence" of the relation to *Autrui* is *au-delà de l'essence*—is betrayal "itself," or is that which undermines and hollows out all real relations. This is precisely how the other person obligates me: *for this other person is without relation,* is alone and mortal, is already beyond my powers and, therefore, I, too, am without relation. Hence my anxiety, and hence the "restlessness" in the self of which Levinas so often speaks. What "binds" me to the other person is the *nonrelation* to the Other, the nothing or no-relation that I, myself, *am.* My skin, a Nessus tunic.

We are describing, then, an ethics of betrayal. But betrayal of what? Of nothing. Of no relation. Betrayal of that relation that can only be betrayed. Betrayal of that "no ethics" that finitude is. For I *am* that finitude that defines and therefore escapes me. That is what makes ethical intentionality an exposure. There is no realizable relation to the other that would be ethical through and through. There will only have been a fictioned, imagined relation—fragile as an image is fragile, ungraspable, unpossessible—a reality made up of nothingness. Outside any particular, defined relation to the other, there is this exposure to "no relation at all" that is an obsession with *Autrui* and that both orients and escapes me. In the end this relation is finitude itself; but it is read by Levinas as something like ethics.

No One Other

Diachrony is the refusal of conjunction, the non-totalizable, and, in this sense, infinite. But in the responsibility for the other, for another freedom, the negativity of this anarchy, this refusal of the present, of appearing, of the immemorial, commands me and ordains me to the other, to the first one on the scene, and makes me approach him, makes me his neighbor.

It diverges from nothingness as well as from being. It provokes this responsibility against my will, that is, by substituting me for the other as a hostage. All my inwardness is invested in the form of a despite-me, for-another. Despite me for another is signification par excellence. And it is the sense of the "oneself," that accusative that derives from no nominative; it is the very fact of finding myself while losing myself.

[La diachronie, c'est le refus de la conjonction, le non-totalisable et, en ce sens précis, Infini. Mais dans la responsabilité pour Autrui—pour une autre liberté—la négativité de cette anarchie, de ce refus opposé au présent,—à l'apparaître—de l'immémorial, me commande et m'ordonne à Autrui, au premier venu, et m'approche de lui, me le rend prochain—s'écarte ainsi du néant comme de l'être, provoquant contre mon gré cette responsabilité, c'est-à-dire me substituant comme otage à Autrui. Toute mon intimité s'investit en contre-mon-gré—pour-un-autre. Malgré moi, pour-un-autre—voilà la signification par excellence et le sens du soi-même, du se—accusatif ne dérivant d'aucun nominatif—le fait même de se retrouver en se perdant.][6]

Radical diachrony (or diachrony without any synchrony) allows us to approach the anteriority or *refus opposé au présent* that defines Levinas's ethics. We may compare this to imperious superegoic guilt, but the involvement described above does not derive from my personal and repressed history of desires. Diachrony that eludes all synchrony is instead the trace of the Other *in* me, but "older" than the *moi*. This is clearly no ethics I might ever understand or theorize, for it is above me and prior to me. I am "its" echo. It orders me and *I* do not even obey it. More precisely, I *am* ordered, I *am* oriented, I *am* schematized such that I am obligated to the first other I can find. One may say, beyond Freud and near to Heidegger, that it throws me, -jects me, or casts me before the other and others.

This ethics, then, is "older" than my self and it is disproportionate to *my* powers. *It* is forever strange. I shall never have the measure of it nor equal its demand. No morality can contain this "otherwise" than me and therefore all *my* morality is in question. It demands a Nietzschean affirmation: a going-under or an *Untergeworfenheit* (to combine Nietzsche with Heidegger for a moment) that will be my sub-jection to *Autrui*. This sub-ject, to be sure, is not the modern Cartesian subject delineated by Heidegger,[7] but is instead a radical nascence that withdraws from essence and is extracted from being. This subjection goes "all the way to the laughter that refuses language [jusqu'au rire qui refuse le langage]."[8]

Ethics, for Levinas, is a command that cannot be recalled, that is olamic, forgotten. It is the forgetting that holds me hostage to the Other and that constrains me beyond my powers and my initiative. This forgetting is beyond me for the simple reason that it is not in my power to forget (no one is "able" to forget; forgetting is precisely a lapse in our ability to remember). Thus, forgetting takes me outside egoity. It denucleates the ego, stripping it nude. I am originally a third-person neuter whom *I* forget (because forgetting, outside egoity, is a forgetting of the *one who* forgets; the "subject" of the forgetting remains always anonymous and is thus preeminently forgettable). My relation to the Other prior to my self is, as it were, contracted by this one who is forgotten, and who forgets. And the relation he (the anonymous *il*, the Neuter) contracts is likewise forgotten, along with the Other.

It calls then from my prehistory, from before my origin, from an immemorial time when I, in my "extreme youth," am not yet present. It calls and it is *It*, i.e., no one that can be known—an Other beyond my powers of identification. Therefore it (or, *It*) is that *from which I cannot distinguish myself.* The very anonymity of *Autrui* is what is so commanding, so imperious, so confounding. Precisely *no one* commands me, no one at all, and therefore no one from whom I can separate myself. Nothing obligates me and therefore I cannot distance myself from obligation—for I *am* it. I *am* ordered, I *am* obligated, in short: *I am Autrui.* It is beyond my power to distinguish myself from this anonymity and thus the identification—the election or the substitution—will already have taken place. It is *I* who calls, that is to say, *no one other.*[9]

You see, responsibility for Levinas is just this unpower of identification prior to myself, prior to any desire, to any motive or interest, to any empiric guilt. For Levinas I *am* only insofar as I am *other*, only insofar as I am identified/substituted for this other, this no one, this no one other than I. Hence the enigma, the "knot [nœud]" in ipseity that philosophy is forced to think.[10] The Other obsesses me because I *am* that Other, who is no one, no other, no one other than my self *it*self. As Levinas puts it: "[T]he psyche in the soul is the other in me, a malady of identity, both accused and *self*, the same for the other, the same by the other [le psychisme de l'âme, c'est l'autre en moi; maladie de l'identité—accusée et *soi*, le même pour l'autre, même par l'autre]."[11]

Ethics, in Levinas's sense, is the very event of the self. It (ethics, the self) happens *to* me, *as* me. The self (always already involved with the Other) comes to me from an outside all the more exterior in that it precedes any interiority. A vertiginous interpellation forms the enigmatic "knot" that is the self or the *ipse*. Radically outside, prior to any inside, this identification, this *trauma*, is just as radically "forgotten." Yet, it *is* me: in me/beyond me. I *incarnate* that which calls me to myself. That is why Levinas can say that ethics "is the breakup of the originary unity of transcendental apperception, that is, it is the beyond of experience [c'est l'éclatement de l'unité originaire de l'aperception transcendentale—c'est-à-dire l'au-delà de l'expérience]."[12] I am, as it were, constitutionally unable not to anonymously incarnate alterity, and here, in a strange way, an ethics is inscribed—*and exscribed*. The self is responsibility incarnate. The very anonymity of alterity—its nothingness, if you will—is the *impossibility of my indifference to it*. All the ego's powers of (oedipal) identification and comprehension are shadowed by this anterior unpower.

In *Otherwise than Being or Beyond Essence*, Levinas describes a subjectivity that precisely withdraws from automanifestation, and he characterizes this withdrawal—or, as he might say, this humility—as the very *autrement qu'être* that ethics "is." The Levinasian subject eludes that which is essential to subjectivity: self-certain presence to self in either its Cartesio-Heideggerian confinement to (auto)representation,[13] or its retrenchment, after Michel Henry, as autoaffection.[14] This novel subject of Levinas's withdraws, then, from the very concept of subjectivity into an enigma that makes the retention of the word abusive. That which is, for Levinas, *hypokeimenon*, underlying, or sub-jacent is that which enters into no present at all and is thus beyond speculation. A strange subject. An image of the subject, one is tempted to say. A strange subject strange to itself since it is always on the "hither side" of representation, but not purely and simply absent. It *is* its aversion to light. It is "an extreme shyness," as Levinas says somewhere. Outside any concept of it, it is exposed, vulnerable, naked. It is *who* I am and it is not, or not simply, my vulnerability to disappearance—to death, to my inability to be there anymore. This subject, as Levinas never tires of telling us, is not destined to appear, and is foreign to any "place in the sun." It is paralyzed: *always already* no longer able to be there anymore. It is, as Levinas tells us (in words that should remind us of his description of the work of art), a "death-like passivity [une passivité à mort]."[15] It "is" nothing other than this surrender of manifestation. The Other occupies its place fully, insisting on the subject's removal from its own manifestation.

For Levinas, the self is *"a deposing of the ego, less than nothing as uniqueness [dé-position du Moi, le moins que rien comme unicité]."*[16] According to Levinas, I have always already abandoned all for-myselfness. I do not first establish for myself a place in the sun and then, as a monadic Archimedean point, fall in with others in one way or another. Subjectivity here is nothing but a primordial delay behind the Other. This is *absolute* passivity (i.e., not relative to any activity, but passivity absolutized as other than, or overwhelming, the difference between active and passive).

The Western metaphysical subject, then, according to Levinas, had been incorrectly conceptualized. It was never meant to come to presence, and therefore it was meant entirely for the Other who shall eternally precede it. The subject would be forever devoted to an obligation that would forever exceed it, since this obligation would define the interiority it is. The crisis into which modernity had fallen, the crisis of the absence of foundations, the discovery that there was no ground beneath our feet, was no crisis at all. It was the belated discovery of a beneficence that had enraptured us beyond ourselves. Our very inability to "unite all the faculties" and to present ourselves to ourselves in the full light of a knowing was, in fact, a "golden opportunity" to overturn all thinking that originates subjectivity in automanifestation or autoaffection.[17]

The philosophical obsession with the subject brought us, despite ourselves and despite our anguish, face-to-face, not with ourselves, but with an alterity that would infinitely postpone autonomy. An extreme humility and an unprecedented ethics had ruined the grand epoch of the Subject and its maniacal striving after itself. Only the language of ethics would be equal to this abyss into which the human sciences had fallen. Even the language of psychoanalysis, which promised a Copernican revolution that would undermine all thinking founded in a Cartesian *Cogito*, had slipped into myth and had remained imprisoned by a classical schema of the subject. As Nancy and Lacoue-Labarthe (and later Borch-Jacobsen) have made clear, the ego's shadow remained, in psychoanalysis from Freud to Lacan, another ego behind the ego, and below the subject there lurked another subject—of desire (or even, of a desire to be a subject).[18] Only the language of ethics would be able to say that that which philosophy was unable to present to itself was not meant to be presented at all. The new *ethical* subject would remain offstage, in the shadows, *en deçà du temps*, and would suffer affectively all that the ego would contract in all its adventures in the world. Ethical subjectivity is infinite vulnerability. The absence of foundation was in fact already a rapport. There was already an exposure to the Other interrupting any beginning. Against all our expectations and prejudices, the subject was not a ground at all. It was unpower and weakness, and this is the case for a simple and even banal reason: the self does not form itself. It has no ability at all until the other and others intervene and bring it into existence. The self is an absolute dependency, and its dependency is an inexhaustible *potentia*.

The Self

The oneself cannot form itself; it is already formed with an absolute passivity. In this sense it is the victim of a persecution that paralyses any assumption that could awaken it so that it would posit itself for-itself. This passivity is that of an attachment that has already been made, as something irreversibly past, prior to all memory and recall. It was made in an irrecuperable time which the present, represented in recall, does not equal, in a time of birth or creation, of which nature or creation retains a trace, unconvertible into a memory.

[Le soi-même ne peut pas *se* faire, il est déjà fait de passivité absolue, et, dans ce sens, victime d'une persécution paralysant toute assomption qui pourrait s'éveiller en lui pour le poser *pour* soi, passivité de l'attachement déjà nouée comme irréversiblement passée, en deça de toute mémoire, de tout rappel. Nouée dans un temps irrécupérable que le présent, représenté dans le rappel n'égale pas, dans un temps de la naissance ou de la création dont nature ou créature garde une trace, inconvertible en souvenir.][19]

The self, enigmatically, "suffers" itself. It is a wound that does not heal. Before myself, prior to any desire to be, anterior to any objectivity, to any distance or any time—literally *ex nihilo*—the self happens to me. The self, the ipse, the *who* that I am (as opposed to the what) *is formed*. It is made, fashioned, begotten, willed, fictioned. Using the language of Levinas, it is wounded and persecuted. The Other has access to me before I do. In-myself, I am a weakness and a dependency. A supplement, in Derrida's sense, is required for me to be a someone and thus the subject cannot be thought outside *différance*. The supplement is a trauma that precedes the constituted ego and therefore precedes all memory and repression. A "forgetting" precedes all remembering and a contact with the outside precedes all interiority. The ego proper—the formed, bounded, healthy, articulated identity—is not its own. It receives itself from without itself (in every sense). Anterior to being-formed, it *is* not. It is undifferentiated, pure exteriority—not even the fragmentation of an unknown embodiment. It is *It*—no one, nothing. Its *self* is borrowed, eaten, absorbed from others. Its self *proper* is not its own, for in-itself it is a "non-quiddity, no one, clothed in purely borrowed being, which makes it a nameless singularity by conferring on it a role [non-quiddité—personne—revêtue d'un être de pur emprunt, qui masque sa singularité sans nom en lui conférant un rôle]."[20] The oneself itself is no one (singular and undifferentiated) who is someone (a self, but a borrowed or stolen one—a someone Other who for that reason sinks into immemoriality in the pre-history of the subject). *Autrement qu'être* is the being-formed, or the vulnerability to the Other, "older" than the ego and always just prior to any self-presence. Being-created is the incarnation that is the self. The self does not identify, it *is* identified with an identification that remains always just anterior to the self. The self does not consist of that to which it agrees (as C. S. Peirce argues). It consists of its absolutely passive being-formed which makes possible its (ambiguous) ability to identify with others and also to imitate them.

It is by way of this "knot" in subjectivity that Levinas is able to speak the language of ethics and say that the subject is incarnated *as* ethical, whether we like it or not. Subjectivity is responsibility-for-the-other and the Other is involved in subjectivity like a play of limits. Through this *stricto sensu* unthinkable enigma, he can say that the human is not at all wolfish but is, from the beginning, for-the-other because its self comes *from* the other who thus robs the subject of all for-itselfness. (Keep this in mind as we conclude the chapter on Agamben, for his politics also relies on a primordial "theft.") What "remains" of me after this trauma is an exceptional obligation to the Other whom I, in fact, incarnate. Only a brusque resentment against the very motif of primordial passivity could possibly ignore what is in fact a commonplace of human existence. No one is born into the world from out of one's own self.

This enigmatic birth, incarnation, and involvement with others prior to myself, this vertiginous identification, accounts for, among other things, the insistence of anarchy in all human intersubjectivity and also the hyperbologic that governs the ego's superegoic guilt. That is, since it is precisely "myself" that I owe to the Other and others, only *complete* being-for-the-other (or, as Levinas sometimes calls it, "maternity") can answer to the demand "inside" me. But as it will always be *I* who am for-the-other, a remainder or trace of for-myselfness is uneradicable, no matter how noble or "selfless" I try to be. Hence, "the more just I am, the more guilty I am [plus je suis juste—plus je suis coupable]."[21] In his way, Levinas has deconstructed the mysterious authority of Freudian superegoic guilt by placing it outside its mythic oedipal triangulation. It is not some figure, some person, from the subject's past that has internally modeled and modified the subject. Levinasian *Autrui* will never have been identified yet will never be without identity, for *I am Autrui* myself, and outside this identification, I am NOTHING. Not even desire. And therefore, I am, in myself, anxiously unfigurable and an-archic. Strangely, paradoxically, but perfectly rigorously, my very *self* is beyond me, is without essence, is otherwise than (my) being. The self is *fairé*: born, begotten, incarnated-as-modeled, copied, echoed, repeated. An anonymous mimesis precedes and permanently erodes all identity. My being is not my own. It is being-possessed, being-cast (in both senses: like a die is thrown, and as if cast into some role in a drama). Using the language of Heidegger, we would say that, for Levinas, *Mit-sein* is *rigorously* correlative with *Da-sein* and *Da-sein's* anxiety (which subtends all its ontic affects) is precisely its lostness in *das Man* since, outside its lostness, it is nothing.

I am haunted, altered—but by no one, no father, no mother. I am haunted by no one other than myself. This is my ungrounded, abyssal, endless passivity. My self comes to me as the very event of my being and therefore, as cast, I am exposed to, and permeated by, alterity. Missing from me, the hole in my being that Hegelo-Kojèvean psychoanalysis after Lacan insists on, is not, as is said, my *self*. The self is *Other*, not lacking. What is "lacking," if that is the word for it, is the for-itselfness proper to the self. The self is an other *(je est un autre)* and therefore is never for-itself, but is "despite-itself-for-another."

We may recognize in this formidable enigma the inspiration for Mikkel Borch-Jacobsen's incessant correction of Freud's notion of primary identification. In *The Freudian Subject*, Borch-Jacobsen is able to point out, by identifying innumerable aporias in Freud's logic and analyses, that, despite the stubbornly held notion of an absolute Narcissus, there is no subject *prior to* "its" identifications. The ego itself then would be both and neither itself and other, or, as Borch-Jacobsen so nicely puts it, would be a *point d'autrui:* a hypnotic and somnambulistic contraction of otherness into sameness.[22] Hence my undecidability with regard to myself—my debts and my guilt, my paranoia and my endless rivalries with others. Borch-Jacobsen is able to show that that at which psychoanalysis aimed—the individual, the ego—was without a self of its own, was "without qualities."[23] The ego had no being of its own and this led Borch-Jacobsen to lead Freud ineluctably from individual to social psychology. For *It* (the id, the unconscious) began to resemble nothing so much as a crowd, a primordial anarchic band. The id, having no being of its own, like the crowd or horde, is always already in-itself outside-itself. It is formlessness "itself" and it is a threat of formless-ness, a threat of the dissolution of the social bond.

What Borch-Jacobsen concludes, or forces Freud to con-clude, is that *It* (the id, the unconscious) is not another subject (of representation) buried in repression and speaking in hieroglyphs, but is instead nothing other than the nascent incompletion and the original passivity of the ego itself. Hence-forth, he concludes, there could be no rigorous Freudian dis-tinction between individual and social psychology, between Same and Other. To use the language of Levinas, the nonplace *(non-lieu)* where I encounter the Other *(Autrui)* in a past im-memorial, outside concepts, is precisely myself *itself*.

This does not mean that the Other has been reduced to the Same. What Levinas argues, and what Borch-Jacobsen brilliantly exploits in his reading of Freud, is that the Same is no longer itself. It is "in question." Levinas has allowed us to read the Same as pure radical exposure to alterity, as infil-trated by alterity. In his introduction to Borch-Jacobsen's book, François Roustang says, concisely, that subjectivity is radically altered and "is never itself except because it is altered, be-cause it is other to itself, because it is its own other, although it is never able to represent that other to itself."[24] And this will forever precede all its dialectical adventures. Outside its birth, it is not an immanence invisible to itself (as in a Hegelian formu-lation). The self is no one, nothing—already both with and with-out rapport with the Other. As supplemented, the self is schema-tized, ordered, categorized as for-the-other or *as (the) rapport itself*. But, this rapport is a communication with no one since the Other is incarnated *in* the self, *as* the self. Nonetheless, the rapport remains. It is never repressed. It is imaginary.

So, if Levinas has given us anything to think it is this: there is no sociality, no community, no communication, no dialogue nor dialectic that is unaffected by a nothingness, an anonymity, a dissymmetry and hence a disproportion, a panic, a restlessness or a delirium at the heart of which there is a subject in *une passivité à mort.*

Impasse

As a result of its originary passivity, of its being formed, the self is delayed "behind" itself. But, as it is nothing other than its passivity, we must conceive of the self *as* delay itself, or—time. Like the work of art, the temporality of the self is without a present. As modeled or doubled or echoed from the Other, the self is "originally" a recurrence to self. The delay is, in the language of ethics, an originary *politesse*, or an "after you, sir." The self is belated, behind the Other and answering to the Other who precedes it. Ex nihilo I respond to the Other before even hearing the Other, before recognizing the Other *as* other. I am thus indistinguishable from that Other.

In spite of what Levinas says here and there, there can be no revelation of this "hither side" of representation. The passivity and vulnerability Levinas insists on are other than I, other than something that is in my power to accomplish. I can no more form my self than I can forget my self. Like forgetting, being-formed is a lapse in power. This lapsing is the *radical* diachrony of which we have already spoken: diachrony without synchrony or, to say the same thing, diachrony as perpetual defection from the present. The self as this delay is subjected to the Other and thus cannot resist being-altered since it is nothing other than being-altered. Subjectivity (being subjected to the other) is a dividing of the past from the future but without passing into a present. Subjectivity, in Levinas's sense, is that which withdraws from "between" past and future. It is time without any "now" point, if that is imaginable. Instead of a "now" point there is a *point d'autrui*—a point of instability and dissolution. Subjectivity, in this sense, is the breakdown of the difference between Same and Other, the breakdown of intersubjectivity, and a proximity to the Other outside of, or evacuated of, any presence. The impossibility of indifference we spoke of earlier is the fact that, in a real case, we cannot doubt that another person is in pain (to borrow from Wittgenstein's work for a moment). It is a fact that gives no information, no content, no ethical formula. It is an affect, but an affect without a self, for I *am* the other from whose suffering I cannot distance myself by doubting. But I do not identify with that sufferer as someone in particular. I identify, very much to the contrary, insofar as the sufferer is *not* other-than-I, is *not* alter ego. That is, I identify insofar as the other is precisely no one in particular, is beyond himself and is not equal to his suffering. *I identify with the other precisely to the extent that the other is anonymous, and thus I identify with no one.* It is only with great difficulty that we can say, with Levinas, that an "ethics" or a "hither side" is revealed here, that a responsibility or an obligation is born here. We can just as easily say that nothing is revealed here. That which the sufferer and I share or have in common—our "common subjectivity" as Bataille puts it (or our being-in-common, as Nancy says)—is precisely NOTHING. No bond. No ethics. No morals. And it is precisely to NOTHING that I cannot remain indifferent. The other, the sufferer, can drag me, despite myself, into that NOTHING that we "share." The affect then, would be, as Blanchot puts it, an "experience of nonexperience," or an incomplete experience, or an experience of the noncompletion that I myself am, that the self is.

For Levinas, this incompleteness *is* myself—or is given to me as that which singularizes me and calls me to myself and to my responsibility. It calls me, in the end, to "thematization, thought, history, and inscription [thématisation, pensée, histoire et écriture]."[25] In other words, like the self, with the self, *as* the self, ethics is born ex nihilo—from its own absence. Ethics is born from the absence of any proper subjective relation. It is born from anxiety. From finitude. There is NOTHING that founds the social order and that is the incessant murmuring I "hear" calling me out of nothing to be someone. Ethics is nothing and hence it is disproportionate, vertiginous, and anxious. This nothing murmurs to me through the Other from whom I am unable to distinguish myself and this blind rapport reveals (without revealing) a for-the-other-for-nothing, or a gratuity, an absurdity, or an insane laughter, that lacerates the for-itself and exposes it to nothing, to death—to that absolute passivity I share with the other. For, I *am* that Other who is then no one other or no other than myself. Insofar as I am identifying with no one, I too am no one. Thus, *I* am not ethical, *I* do not substitute. The impossibility of indifference in the scene of suffering is also an inability to say *I*.

The event of ethics that happens to me is also the interruption of ethics. I can no more reveal or represent this ethics than I can imagine myself dead or absent from myself. Ethics, the response to another in pain, is a repetition of my birth—a repetition of that repetition that I *am*, of the echo the self *is*. Levinasian ethics is the "presentation" of myself to myself as repetition (i.e., as unpresentable). The impasse we wish to describe, then, is my becoming self or my coming to myself as repetition or recurrence. The subject is nothing outside of its return to itself. The subject is radically no one, is imaginary, is "clothed in purely borrowed being," or is given, as Lacoue-Labarthe says of *Da-sein*, "the gift of nothing."[26] The subject is without qualities, blank, and thus infinitely unstable. At the same time, as no one, the subject is deeply panicked, paranoid, a man of crowds, at home nowhere—for the Other has stolen him from himself at birth. I am and I am not who I am. In short, we come very close here to madness, or something like madness.

Ethics will have been born where it was dissolved: in primal (a)sociality where "each one is the other and no one is himself," as Heidegger describes *das Man*. In a sense, Levinas wishes to say that this is our "proper" state: "Paradoxically it is qua *alienus*—foreigner and other—that man is not alienated [Paradoxalement, c'est en tant qu'alienus—étranger et autre—que l'homme n'est pas aliéné]."[27] For Levinas, being is being-cast, being-enrolled, being-dramatized. Being *is* (simultaneously) "otherwise than being." Being-cast is inspiration by the other and delay behind the present: a diachrony. Between *Geworfenheit* and *Verfallenheit* is being-cast, being-formed, being-ficted—the (imaginary) space of literature, in other words. *Geworfenheit* and *Verfallenheit* are, therefore, strictly correlative. There is no chronology, no fall from grace into thrownness (or, into articulation). My "fallenness" into the "they" *is* the revelation of the nullity I am. Thus, being-cast, in a certain sense, precedes both fallenness and thrownness. It "throws" me into thrownness, or articulates it. Fallenness is always already articulated as thrownness.

But "otherwise than being" is not, or not strictly, ethical. It is also the suspension of ethics. There is no "scene" of enigmatic rapport that can be displayed before us. *Da-sein* and the Levinasian subject do not simply "fall," they are vertiginously articulated, singled out, and elected.

Éthique

The reality of the other person, of *Autrui*, is, as Levinas says of Proust's Albertine, made up of time, of evanescence, if you like—of nothingness. That which is other in the other person is otherness "itself": the radical temporality of a diachrony without synchronic horizon, or, in a word, *dying*. *Autrui* is constituted as and by that which only escapes. Because of this, not in spite of it, we come to be involved with the other intimately *as* other, outside of any concept or thought of the other.

In the writings of Emmanuel Levinas the language of ethics has come to designate (one is tempted to say, has come to the rescue of) a singular, counteruniversal, nonintentional (that is to say, aimless, purposeless, nonconscious) relation with and response to the other person *as* other (and not as alter ego, another version of the same, nor, for that matter, as a self at all). This strange ethics (and it is quite precisely strange—it is a singular relation, unique, unrecognizable, and, like the result of a dice throw, does not relate to other relations) is realized as a "substitution of me for the others [substitution de moi aux autres],"[28] and it can only be included in any morality, politics, or community whatever *as excluded* (or, as Levinas puts it, as "betrayed"). This means that any proper relationship with another already betrays what is "essentially" a rapport without essence or an impropriety that precedes and makes possible (while at the same time making questionable) any relationship whatever. That which constitutes ethics, for Levinas, is the "loss" of propriety—or its absence, or its presence-as-betrayed. It is a loss that precedes there being anything to lose, or it is a relation "with" loss that suggests the very possibility any relation whatever. In any case, it is impossible to say simply and unequivocally that which Levinas has given us to think, that which any ethics outside essence demands.

Giorgio Agamben puts it this way:

The fact that must constitute the point of departure for any discourse on ethics is that there is no essence, no historical or spiritual vocation, no biological destiny that humans must enact or realize. That is the only reason why something like ethics can exist, because it is clear that if humans were to be this or that substance, this or that destiny, no ethical experience would be possible—there would only be tasks to be done.

[Il fatto da cui deve partire ogni discorso sull'etica è che l'uomo non è ne ha da essere o da realizzare alcuna essenza, alcuna vocazione storica o spirituale, alcun destino biologico. Solo per questo qualcosa come un'etica può esistere: poiché è chiaro che se l'uomo fosse o avesse da essere questa o quella sostanza, questo o quel destino, non vi sarebbe alcuna esperienza etica possible—vi sarebbero solo compiti da realizzare.][29]

The "point of departure" here is in fact the absence of anything that would constitute a point of departure, which is why ethics will always have been, as Agamben puts it, "something like ethics." There will be something *like* ethics because there will be no ethics *proper*. The "ethical experience," to be possible at all, presupposes no essence nor any destiny that would have this or that designation. That is to say, the "ethical experience," outside essence, will be an experience of an improper, incoherent, indeterminate obligation. Outside any proper or authentic relation to the other, the very presence of the other person will be drained of substance, and the subject will find itself in a singular relation to the Other without measure or comparison. At the limit of any community or any relation whatever, Levinas wishes to reveal a proximity that cannot be made present, but that I cannot divorce myself from. The ethics Levinas has in mind is one that "happens" to me when another person loses his or her proper relation to him- or herself. This erosion of presence constitutes an event (or, better, *is* the event of the emptying out of all presence) that "denucleates" the self *(moi)*, and thus the relationship proper with the other person slips into a vertigo, an inducement, a provocation, or a suggestion—something *like* an ethical obligation, but only imprecisely, loosely. In fact it is impossible to characterize what "happens" here and it is only ambiguously that the language of ethics is "equal to," or is the meaning of, this erosion.[30] It is Levinas's project to show that all human relations are always threatened by an evacuation of presence, and he insists on our ethical obligation to "the next one I meet," the next one on the street I happen to run into. What Levinas wants to say is that human life is in rapport with a *general* impropriety that suggests both anarchy *and* community, both stability *and* instability. That is to say, according to Levinas, there is a relation in relation to which I am always already in relation, or in relation to which I am absolutely passive. This passivity is a response to the Other—beyond him- or herself—that I come to be responsible for. But, and this is strange, responsible *for nothing* (that is to say, *not* necessarily responsible to restore the other to propriety, for that would presuppose some common essence or destiny). It is a responsibility propriety cannot satisfy.

We return again and again to this fragile and indefinable relation with *Autrui* as *that from which I cannot distinguish myself*. Beyond or otherwise than doubt or certainty, this singular relation (resembling ethics and rendering ethics a resemblance to itself, that is, denucleating it of essence) is anarchy—the coming (apart) of any community whatever. It happens to us when, for example, another person is in pain, or for that matter, in ecstasy. It happens when another person is deprived of the dignity of the self, as when death approaches, or as when someone forgets himself in passion. Dispossessed of self, outside oneself, the other person is, if we may say this, possessed *by* dispossession, or by anonymity. In the grips of pain or passion the other person, no longer him- or herself, is no longer self-possessed and something irreparable happens. This occurred, as we know, to Bataille, who became so obsessed with the famous photograph of a man who was being flayed and dismembered while being kept conscious with opium. The expression on the sufferer's face, Bataille says, was "at once ecstatic(?) and intolerable."[31] The other person became unsimple: neither simply living nor dead, neither in pain nor in ecstasy—became, we may say, communication between these poles—no longer a self but communication "itself." This event of communication may happen to us when someone (like one of the glamorous people from the film *Paris Is Burning*) is engaged in the project of passing from male to female, or the reverse. There the other person passes beyond mere imitation of female (or male) and approaches, not a third sex, but the communication between the sexes that makes that which is called gender possible, while calling it into question. In these extravagant cases, the other person becomes radically dis-placed, seems to belong nowhere, seems to have lost a world, and becomes, as Levinas puts it, "naked beyond nudity" because this "someone" will have exceeded any localizable contexts. When this happens, all proper relations to the other are suspended and there is, before anything else, a fascination. This fascination or obsession is the "substance" of Levinas's ethics.[32]

With a Blanchotian accent, Levinas had given us to understand that, before it is anything else, our relation with the
other person is an involuntary fascination. *Autrui* is arresting
and paralyzing. We can be overcome by, or experience, an
arresting fascination with another person who has "passed
beyond" while remaining here. It is a fascination with that
which presents itself as outside itself—as drained of all reality,
as threatened or already contaminated by absence, but in such
a way that presence and absence cease to be the proper terms
for the Other. The other person, outside any simple presentation, is "beyond" while remaining here, before me; but this
"here" is no longer a presence, it is, as it were, delayed behind
itself, or is yet to come. It is the *un*presence of communicativity.
The other person is threatened with becoming a spectacle—a
reality made up of nothingness (as, for example, in professional wrestling, where the spectacle comes from the draining
away of all "real" wrestling and competition). The face-to-
face rapport from *Totality and Infinity* is such a spectacular
relation. There, the other person, as *visage*, is presented as
made up of that passing away that does not pass: time. (In
professional wrestling, all reality having been drained away,
something yet remains to be seen. That which is arresting is
always that which remains to be seen while all is already in
front of me, but as if yet to come.) Beyond any proper relation
to self, a spectacle comes to arrest and paralyze us: that to
which there is no proper response. And the paralysis we feel is
a paralysis *of the subject*. Bataille probably knew this better
than anyone: "A man alive, who sees a fellow-man die, can
survive only *beside himself* [s'il voit son semblable mourir, un
vivant ne peut plus subsister que *hors de soi*]."[33]

One does not merely observe a scene here. For, when the
other person is drained of all substance, when his reality *is*
this erosion, when *Autrui* faces us like "the next one I meet"

(like a stranger, in other words), then the borders between stage and audience are suspended and we are "involved," "elected," "singularized." The paralysis of the subject is an uncontrollable rapport with the other person. With this is carried away all proper difference between Same and Other. There is an identification of the Same with the Other that denucleates the Same of sameness and renders the other person all the more Other in that I am the same as he (who, nonetheless, remains other than I, other than anyone). This is an intimacy more profound than sympathy or empathy, which presuppose a stability in the Same who *can* identify with the other. What happens in Levinasian proximity is an inability or a nonintentionality that seizes us from the inside. This loss of propriety is contagious. It is shared like a communal ecstasy.

Anonymous identification is not a knowledge that I too can die, or that I too can have my gender transformed. It is an experience of anonymity (an experience in the absence of there being anyone there to have the experience). It is the experience of being *already* dead. Anonymous identification is a paralysis that subjects me to alterity "despite myself," and this is the very structure of subjectivity for Levinas: despite-oneself-for-another.

It is precisely this singular response or "relation"—paralyzing and anonymous, "despite-me"—that Levinas seeks to appropriate to the language of ethics. He wishes to define ethics as an anonymous involvement with alterity that calls for and dissolves all proper relations with the other person, and it "poses problems if one is not to abandon oneself to violence. It calls for comparison, measure, knowing, laws, institutions—justice [à moins de s'abandonner à la violence, pose des problems. Elle en appelle alors à la comparaison, à la mesure, au savoir, aux lois, aux institutions—à la justice]."[34] That is to say, outside pure and simple abandonment to violence, to a

Hobbesian war of all against all, there must be something like knowing, laws, justice, and so forth—all of which must remain questionable and retain within themselves a call for their revaluation. There is no ethics proper, per se, or as such anywhere in Levinas's works. But neither is there a pure and simple absence of ethics. The call of the Other will never cease to place an incoherent demand in the soul of the subject to which no response is adequate (by definition, for nothing can be adequate to the incoherent). His ethics, therefore, is, as he says, an "obsession." Every response to the other, every restoration to the general, will betray the demand. But at the same time, each betrayal will be a new relation with the other and thus ethics will mime or "conform" to mimesis, to the improper "itself." There will be no reaching ethics, no teaching it, no instituting it. There will be instead the slow emptying out of any determinate relation whatsoever, and this emptying out will articulate by exhaustion and exclusion the singular "itself." This does not mean that ethics is any relation at all. Any relation at all would remain just that—indifferent—were it not for the peculiar gravity of mimesis: that to which *no* relation (and no language) is adequate.

Levinas's ethics, if it is ethics, will be an experience of this impossibility: there is no relation that is either inside or outside the obligation to respond to the Other that is not also a substitution of me for the other. Substitution, in Levinas, is the very measure of a measureless weakness: finitude. That is to say, there is no human relation that does not circumscribe a loss that passes without passing away. That loss is inscribed in, or as, the face of the other person who faces me from beyond himself and thereby obligates that I am called on to be substituted for him *who cannot substitute for himself*, and who is abandoned to an infinite vulnerability that it is beyond his power to equal (abandoned beyond even any violence that may be done to him)—like the man tortured to death in China who so obsessed Bataille. In the face of the other, in the spectacle that is an image losing its reference, is the presentation of the impossibility of finitude: the Other, precisely, cannot be *himself*. *Autrui* cannot be himself and therefore I am called to be for-him. He is not equal to himself, by definition, as Heidegger has so implacably shown. That is how it is with the other person, and that is why he obsesses me. He is weak, impoverished, homeless, glorious . . . That is what affects me beyond characterization and beyond description. Even the homeless are not equal to their homelessness—they are always worse off or otherwise affected than others (or they themselves) can say they are. Those who suffer cannot grasp their suffering, even if they tell us of it. On the "hither side" of all that is said, an infinite vulnerability obsesses us beyond measure.

Ethics, as Levinas defines it, is rigorously correlative with finitude. The paralysis of the subject is the infinite vulnerability that *is* finitude—its openness to any relation whatever (just or unjust, responsible or not). And, there is no ethics of finitude. There is something like a suggestion, a murmur that obliges us and constrains us to something *like* ethics. Something, however, that will always have "duped" us in the sense of our having been taken in by a dubious scheme in spite of our best (or worst) intentions. Something will always have dragged us against our will into a vertigo from which only a nameless and affectless voice will speak, like the narrative voice from Blanchot.[35]

Death
The space of radical ethics—a relation with others that precedes egology—is deeply, even definitively, ambiguous. As ambiguous, it is neutral and neutralizing. It is as much a

space of death and dying, of finitude, literature, and madness, as it is of ethics. Finitude is given at birth by the Other whom I forget but to whom I owe the finitude I am. I am ignorant of my birth as I am of my death, since these define and therefore escape me, or involve me in a limit over which I exercise no control. It is (the) Other(s) who involve(s)[36] me in these limits that define me. Only by an abuse of language, however, can this space be appropriated to the language of ethics; for the space of incarnation and death is singular and incomparable. It belongs to no one. It is properly neither ethical nor aesthetic. It is no more the first sign of ethics (an extreme humility before the other) than of histrionics (the ability to play all the roles with an icy detachment), or of madness (a dispossession of self and a repossession by who knows what forces or demons). Incarnation is irreducibly undecidable, unoccupiable, and unpresentable. But this is also the space of existence which is, as Nancy says, "offered by no one to no one." It is offered, but it is always already lost or surrendered because it belongs to no one. It is, Nancy says, "shared," but only as that which eludes all sharing.[37] There can be no transcending this space, since it is unequal or insufficient to itself. Therefore, as Blanchot reminds us:

> It does not follow, however, that the community is the simple putting in common, inside the limits it would propose for itself, of a shared will to be several, albeit to do nothing, that is to say, to do nothing else than maintain the sharing of 'something' which, precisely, seems always already to have eluded the possibility of being considered as part of a sharing: speech, silence.

> [La communauté n'est pas pour autant la simple mise en commun, dans les limites qu'elle se tracerait, d'une

volonté partagée d'être à plusieurs, fût-ce pour ne rien
faire, c'est-à-dire ne rien faire d'autre que de maintenir
le partage de 'quelque chose' qui précisément semble
s'être toujours déjà soustrait à la possibilité d'être
considéré comme part à un partage: parole, silence.][38]

This space, without or beyond essence *(au-delà de
l'essence)*, this being-in-common that *is* only as "otherwise
than being," is, for Levinas, the place of a responsibility that
places me in question, for only there, outside essence, *can* I
meet the other as other than other-I. The ambiguity of this
space is shareable only as contested, as in-question (hence, it
is the space not only of responsibility, but also of rivalry and
jealousy). Death is inscribed here as well. It is the space of the
finitude, we must say, in spite of Levinas's profound aversion
to fundamental ontology and Bataille's impatience with Heidegger's "slavish" devotion to philosophy. It is finitude as that
obligation-to-be that I cannot ever meet, for it defines me and
is thus beyond me as the inescapable voice of conscience that
calls *Da-sein* to itself by putting it in question. It is an improper space, belonging to no one, and is given to *Da-sein,*
but only on condition that *Da-sein* is radically no one.

Undifferentiated space is a space of unpower, of anarchy.
It is where there is exposure to exposure. In this space, the
other person, enrolled as this or that member of society (or
part of some whole), is depropriated and communicates with
this space itself—beyond any self. Here the other person is
approached by an unpower over which he can exercise no
mastery and for which his role does not prepare him. Levinas
says, "the face is exposed, menaced, as if inviting us to an act
of violence [le visage est exposé, menacé comme nous invitant
à un acte de violence]."[39] The entire lacerated body of the
man tortured in China, whose photographs Bataille had seen,

was a *visage* in the Levinasian sense. His mutilation excites a passion *for further mutilation*, even as it excites a passionate revulsion. In this space of contestation—of rivalry, of jealousy, of torture, of death—the other person loses himself and "offers" to me an opening into this space. The Other is subject to a withdrawal over which there is no control and of which there is no knowledge. At the same time, he begins to *lose* his ability-to-die, his definitive mortal *potentia*, his "own most" possibility. He begins to lose the possibility that defines him as *Da-sein*. This possibility, Heidegger tells us, once realized is, hence, no longer possible and *Da-sein*, once realized in its being, loses itself absolutely because it is no longer *able* to die. It is to that definitive powerlessness that I respond. This may be the beginning of an ethics, but it would be a fatal one because I am not able to distinguish myself from that powerlessness. The other person is no longer able to forestall the approach of death—a paralysis that, in spite of his language, defines Heidegger's *Entschlossenheit* as a radical passivity. It is to this passivity that exposes beyond nudity that I respond, and for which I am responsible. In its approach (as the possibility-to-die that is already an inability-to-cease-dying), finitude escapes from "between" us, and hence, there is a vertiginous (or anonymous) contact. I identify with this Other nonintentionally, prior to any decision, for there is no one to identify with and nothing to intend. There is an empty identification "despite myself" that interrupts my "as for me."

The response is prior to consciousness and it dissolves the social bond, since I identify with the Other who is no one at all, is already beyond the social. Outside my self, I *am* that Other who, paralyzed and dying, is *already* no longer able to be there anymore. The Other and I share this dying outside ourselves that both touches and separates us. Resoluteness *(Entschlossenheit)* escapes me and is already a response to the

Other who presents (my) death to me by revealing it not to be my death, nor his, nor anyone's. I am obligated to be for-the-other, to die in his place, in that space where the other person is approached by an unpower that approaches me and from which I have no power to separate myself. This is not a communion, nor an exchange of places. It is the corrosive and sobering recognition that the other person is not able to die *his own* death. That is what is so terrible about the final hour. The solitude of dying must be shared.[40] I die for-the-other and in his place because the other cannot. He remains, to the end, uncannily alive, remains unable to cease to die, and surrenders the own-mostness (the possibility to die) that defines him. Death is impersonal. That is why I must be there for him, with him. I am called to accomplish what he cannot accomplish himself. I must substitute for him this ability to die that *I* am. I am that supplement he demands, obliges, in order to *be*, in order to remain possible. However, I offer him what is not my own, what I cannot offer, what I am unable to give. Hence we enter a deathlike passivity *(une passivité à mort)* together. This impossible obligation and impossible relation does not define me as tragic. It exposes me to the radical *inability* that I *must be*—that that to which I am ethically obligated is beyond me, beyond my power. I identify with the other insofar as he is no one, is beyond himself, and therefore I too am beyond, am no one, no *ipse*—am myself already unable to die. To substitute, to supplement for the other, is to die, *like* the other, *as* Other. Just as the other must die a death not his own, so too I must die an other's death. Substitution, the "germ" of Levinas's *Otherwise than Being or Beyond Essence*,[41] is not accomplished except beyond me, outside me, despite-me-for-another. Substituting for the other, I die, thus accomplishing what the other cannot. But dying for-the-other, I remain unable to die my own death. I die away from myself. Death is impersonal; it belongs to no one. Hence, everyone dies an Other's death, no one his own.

The ethics of substitution is betrayed by an internal limit. It is an impasse. I leave the scene. I abandon and betray the Other who calls to me. What remains is the call from no one to no one. A call to which no ethics, no obligation, is adequate. The relation to the Other, like finitude itself, is beyond my grasp. Levinas's ethics is haunted by finitude, the very finitude that *suggests* an ethics. The call of finitude—lacerating me, exposing me, enrolling me, obsessing me—says nothing. It is that *other* death that dispossesses me of myself.

Yet I *must be* this existence, this finitude, which is offered by no one to no one. I *am* nothing—nothing other than that being-offered, that supplement, or that substitution that I cannot accomplish. I *am* Other—that is, no one, no *ipse*. I *am* only as substituted. That is why I am always the first person accused, the first person responsible. My fascinated attentiveness to the Other is the breakup of my unity. The relation to the Other is singular, unique, nongeneralizable. There is no ethics as such, no ethics itself. Or, this ethics is structured like impropriety, and the Levinasian subject is nothing but its infinite unfinished vulnerability.

Levinas and Heidegger

If Levinas's ethics is an elaborate description of finitude, then something about finitude—its primordial temporality, its diachrony, its always-outside-itselfness—suggests to Levinas an ethics. Time itself *means* ethics to Levinas. *Dasein*—that being that does not have its being, that is always in question, that is the "pure abyss of presence in the present"[42]—suggests to Levinas, possibly to us as well, some kind of ethics. If being only "is" in its passing, or in its being-altered, or being-cast, and if *Da-sein* is *Mit-einandersein*, then, letting go of anxiety about lostness (as Bataille recommended), it welcomes the Other. Ethics would be suggested, as if hypnotically, by the call of finitude, if finitude is understood to be rigorously articulated as *Mit-einandersein*.

The space we share/expose is the space of an instability that cannot be commanded. It is the space of a radical contestation of discourses that cannot be rigorously distinguished from each other. It is, if you like, the space of language itself, of writing before the letter, as Derrida says, or of *le dire*, as Levinas prefers. Insofar as Levinas's text comes to double Heidegger's (*diachronie* and *Zeit*, *anarchie* and *das Man*, *le sujet* and *Da-sein*, *responsabilité* and *Gewissenheit*, and so forth) his work amounts to a vast protest against what Heidegger *could* mean, a protest against the appropriation of finitude to "fundamental ontology." In an essay on Lyotard, Lacoue-Labarthe says, "I have a lot of trouble not seeing in Heidegger's 'being', if it is still being, and if it is Heidegger's being, the same thing as (if not its very possibility) Levinas's 'the otherwise than being'. Or as an empty transcendence."[43]

That is, by acting as a competitor to Heidegger and to fundamental ontology, Levinas has exposed and exploited an an-archic rapport and has attempted to undermine Heidegger, who wrote no ethics. Who wrote no ethics for the very good reason that there is nothing adequate or equal to finitude, nothing "otherwise" than finitude. Levinas *is* Heidegger in French, but this can undermine Heidegger in German. In very different ways, Bataille and Levinas each echo Heidegger. Each says what Heidegger will not say because it is unsayable. For Levinas, there is no meaning in the fact that there is no ethics of finitude. By repeating Heidegger in terms of ethics, Levinas gives us nothing to think, nothing to know beyond this suggestion: why did finitude not suggest an ethics to Heidegger?

We do not suggest that Levinas puts his own text in question in order to put Heidegger's text in question. We suggest that the ethics that gnaws at and transfigures Levinas is an involuntary dramatization of being-in-question. We are suggesting that finitude itself is infinitely suggestible. It cannot but suggest a "beyond" or an "otherwise than being." Levinas's ethics, in its way, unleashes this suggestion.

THREE

Blanchot, *L'arrêt de mort,* and the Image of Literature

Artists are replicants who have found the secret of their obsolescence.

—*Massumi*

Writing

Writing obscures that of which it speaks. Yet writing says, each time, clearly and unobtrusively, *there is*. It says this if only to deny it: *there is* not . . . Writing affirms existence—the thing itself, the real—but only by taking its place. Writing takes the place of the real in order to say it. It intrudes itself between us and the reality of which it speaks. Still, outside of writing (before it, prior to it) what has really taken place? What happened? Writing would like to say this thing, but as it sets out to do this it is immediately infected by a foreignness that weakens it immeasurably. Instead of saying the thing, it says (or even, like the work of art in Levinas, it *insists on*) its *absence* by presenting *itself* in the place of that to which it would like to refer. But, what is writing *itself* (outside of, or just short of, its referring to the thing)? And did we not begin this paragraph by saying that writing says, not absence, but existence, *there is?* We should have said: *Writing tears itself apart from the moment it begins to speak.* But who can say this?

Let us go further.

What if existence *is* only as absence, and more precisely,

65

as that absence that writing says, affirms, and "presents"? Or, to say the same thing again, what if existence (the real, the thing itself) is already the *saying of absence*, in short, writing—the very writing whose presence insists upon the absence of the real? In that case writing would be the very taking-place of (double genitive) existence: writing takes the place of existence and existence takes place as writing (but not—and let us be clear about this, for it is a temptation to which Levinas says aesthetic existence is prone—as purely and simply formed or narrated). That which happens outside the text takes place as writing but is not re-presented *in* the text. We could say that writing *is* the very happening of an outside that remains in the text, but only as a silence, like the *voix narrative* of which Blanchot speaks.[1] We could also say that writing "forgets" itself and that this has untold consequences; silence affirms itself in writing without having the strength to say itself.

In our first chapter we saw how in art the crepuscular paroxysmality of naked matter suddenly makes an obscure "appearance." Levinas shows this to us in his evaluation of art from both "La réalité et son ombre" and the section from *Existence and Existents* whose title quietly sums up the unique atmosphere he finds in art: "Existence without a World [Existence sans Monde]."[2] He makes it clear in the later work that the notion of matter that interests him is not some stuff that is utterly refractory to mind, but is instead that matter which can only appear in poetry (but namelessly and without any objectivity).[3] He refers to that aspect of matter which is liberated when, via art, our relations with the world (with usefulness and work) are neutralized. As we have seen in our first chapter, this neutralization is the very event of art and it immerses us in an atmosphere where space is without a horizon, where "[n]aked elements, simple and absolute [Éléments nus, simples et absolus]" detach themselves from things and are "cast towards us like chunks that have weight in themselves [se jettent sur nous des choses comme des morceaux qui s'imposent par eux-mêmes]."⁴ Importantly, this chaotic matter is none other than that matter which is "defined by mechanistic laws which wring out its whole essence and render it intelligible [définie par les lois mécanistes qui en épuisaient et la rendaient intelligible]."⁵ It is not, however, the same *thing* as this *inter-essed* matter. It is not the same thing as matter that is formed, that is some *item* that rests in a setting, a world, and that is, as Heidegger puts it, *zuhandensein*. Aesthetic matter is not destined to the hand, to the subject, or to any user community. It is instead matter destined only to *appear*, and only in poetry, but without being named.

But this other destiny or other aspect to matter is not a new quality that art discovers (and would, thereby, contribute to the intelligibility of the world). It is not a quality that would be poetry's offering to science and philosophy, culture and psychology. That which art discovers, or uncovers, or lays bare will not be found under any encyclopedic subject heading. To put it very simply: art is useless matter. It is made up of useless matter and uselessness is not one of matter's qualities. (It is, Agamben would say, something like a "halo [aureola].")⁶ We may say, however, that uselessness is one of matter's "possibilities." But what does this mean, and what does it mean that only in art does this "possibility" appear as such? Does it mean that art realizes the possibility of uselessness and puts it to work (and thereby betrays it)?

In his essay "Characteristics of the Work of Art," Blanchot says (in terms that are close to both Levinas and Heidegger) that "if the sculptor uses stone and if the road builder also uses stone, the first uses it in a way that it is not used, consumed, negated by usage, but affirmed, revealed in its obscurity, as a road that leads only to itself [si le sculpteur se sert de la pierre et si le cantonnier aussi se sert de la pierre, le premier l'utilise de telle sorte qu'elle n'est pas utilisée, consommée, niée par l'usage, mais affirmée, révélée dans son obscurité, chemin qui ne conduit qu'à elle même]."[7] The artwork, leading the stone, as it were, back to itself (but did it ever leave itself?) "makes what disappears in the object appear [fait apparaître ce qui disparaît dans l'objet]."[8] It is material that disappears into the object, and "the more the material is appropriate—the more it nears nothingness [plus la matière { . . . } est appropriée, plus elle se fait proche de rien]."[9] But in the artwork this matter is preserved. "The statue glorifies the marble," Blanchot says, echoing both Levinas and Heidegger, and the artwork "*is* eminently *that* of which it *is made* [*est* éminemment *ce dont* elle *est faite*]."[10] However,

> The painting is not made from material ingredients added to a canvas; it is the presence of this matter, which without it would remain hidden to us. And the poem likewise is not made with ideas, or with words, it is the point from which words begin to become their appearance, and the *elemental depth* upon which this appearance is opened while at the same time it closes.

> [Le tableau n'est pas fait à partir de la toile et avec des ingrédients matériels, il est la présence de cette matière qui sans lui nous resterait cachée. Et le poème encore n'est pas fait avec des idées, ni avec des mots, mais il est ce à partir de quoi les mots deviennent leur apparence et la *profondeur élémentaire* sur laquelle cette apparence est ouverte et cependant se referme.][11]

The work of art requires materials just like objects do. Plastic, ink, canvas, and marble are necessary to art, and matter can be used in such a way that it vanishes into its uses. But art uses matter such that it is *un*used, workless, idle, useless. Art simply causes the marble to "appear," not to disappear into use. In poetry likewise, words, detached from referentiality, suddenly make a material appearance. It is the appearance of matter that *is*, eminently, what the work of art is made of. Not matter in its thingly reality, but in its appearing *as such*. Not thingliness, but the image of matter. Imaginary matter, if you prefer. It is unemployed matter, or that aspect of matter that remains always prior to its being material *for* this or that. Art *is* unused, unemployed, and idle matter. Art, in short, is the image of matter. I can dismantle the temple and build a road with the marble, but I cannot dismantle the *image* the temple eminently *is*. I can cast celluloid into the fire but I cannot manipulate the motion picture *itself*. I cannot even touch it.

It appears. It disappears. At the same time. For, this image of matter that precedes its disappearance into the object (the thing that settles into the familiar horizons of the world) is not in turn the material for a perception. That is why Blanchot says that the so-called elemental depth is "opened" but "at the same time it closes." Levinas says that "paradoxical as it may seem, painting is a struggle with sight [si paradoxal que cela puisse paraître, la peinture est une lutte avec la vision]" for "sight seeks to draw out of the light beings integrated into a whole [elle cherche à arracher à la lumiére les êtres intégrés dans un ensemble]."[12] Imaginary matter—matter that is its own image and that only appears in poetry (but remains unseen, unobserved, unperceived, silent)—is matter *as such*, in its *ipseity* or origin. (What is *ipseity* if not origin, anteriority, something *as itself, as such*, prior to its predicative involvements in the world?)

Uselessness, we have said, is not a quality. It will not be found in any list of qualities that would distinguish matter. Yet, it is only as useless that matter is made to appear as such, as itself—unformed, unthingly, and unilluminated. Useless, aesthetic matter is neither graphic nor acoustic. To be sure, in the temple marble is revealed as unemployed matter and it can appear, to the industrious engineer, as material for a road (especially since the gods have long since fled the temple and replicant temples made of other materials exist elsewhere as museum pieces, thus rendering the bare existence of this temple superfluous). This is just the point. No one *sees* the useless-ness of matter. One sees material *for* this or that. Materiality *itself* harbors itself in its own visibility. That is its obscurity. In its uselessness, unclothed by forms, it withdraws from percep-tion. When the gods have fled the temple and when even their flight has been forgotten, Blanchot says in this essay, then the temple is no longer a temple and it returns to itself, without ever having departed from itself, in its sheer, obscure, and unperceived presence. It returns to materiality itself, its ori-gin, without any proper name or place in the world. Material-ity (or aesthetic, or imaginary matter) is the name given to matter *itself*—that strange body which has no proper name since its presence remains unperceived. Insofar as it has no purpose and serves no purpose, art affirms this namelessness: the very fact of the *il y a*, as Levinas says.[13] It is an affirmation that deforms all writing and that makes of all writing an ero-sion of that propriety which places the things of the world within our grasp. Such deformed writing would be poetry: the very difference or divergence of the visible from the invisible.

In the renowned passage that immediately follows "Exist-ence without a World," Levinas describes "existence without existents" (which amounts to the same thing, since existents, or beings, belong to a world). He says:

Let us imagine all beings, things, and persons, revert-ing to nothingness. One cannot put this return to noth-

ingness outside of all events. But what of this nothingness itself? Something would happen, if only the night
and silence of nothingness. The indeterminacy of this
'something is happening' is not the indeterminacy of a
subject and does not refer to a substantive. Like the
third person pronoun in the impersonal form of the verb,
it designates not the uncertainly known author of the
action, but the characteristic of this action itself which
somehow has no author. This impersonal, anonymous,
yet inextinguishable "consummation" of being, which
murmurs in the depths of nothingness itself we shall
designate by the term *there is*. The *there is*, inasmuch
as it resists personal form, is 'being in general.'

[Imaginons le retour au néant de tous les êtres: choses
et personnes. Il est impossible de placer ce retour au
néant en dehors de tout événement. Mais ce néant lui-
même? Quelque chose se passe, fût-ce la nuit et la silence du néant. L'indétermination de ce 'quelque chose
se passe,' n'est pas l'indétermination du sujet, ne se
réfère pas à un substantif. Elle désigne comme le
pronom de la troisième personne dans la forme
impersonnelle du verbe, non point un auteur mal connu
de l'action, mais le caractère de cette action elle-même
qui, en quelque matière, n'a pas d'auteur, qui est
anonyme. Cette 'consommation' impersonnelle,
anonyme, mais inextinguible de l'être, celle qui
murmure au fond du néant lui-même, nous la fixons
par le terme d' *il y a*. L'*il y a*, dans son refus de prendre
une forme personnelle, est l' 'être en général'.][14]

This crepuscular event is the writer's most quotidian milieu. As we saw in our first chapter, artists work with images.

They work with that which resists work and which balks at personal form. They work within the imaginary milieu that precedes the world and its interests, a milieu where no one properly belongs. In his famous essay "Two Versions of the Imaginary," Blanchot asks:

> But what is the image? When there is nothing, the image finds in this nothing its necessary condition, but there it disappears. The image needs the neutrality and the fading of the world; it wants everything to return to the indifferent deep where nothing is affirmed; it tends toward the intimacy of what still subsists in the void.

> [Mais qu'est-ce que l'image? Quand il n'y a rien, l'image trouve là sa condition, mais y disparaît. L'image demande la neutralité et l'effacement du monde, elle veut que tout rentre dans le fond indifférent où rien ne s'affirme, elle tend à l'intimité de ce qui subsiste encore dans le vide.][15]

In formulations that have become so familiar to us, we may say that the image, art, or poetry (insofar as poetry begins only when words become their own image) is the presence of absence, the impossibility that nothingness (or death) be present in person. Or, we may say that when everything disappears, disappearance itself "appears." These formulations remain helpful only insofar as we remain attentive to their obscurity, for they do not clarify the notion of an "elemental depth" that Blanchot involves us in. It remains our task to think that it is *in* language, *in* writing, that naked existence is touched, not in the world (in which I continually hide from my exposure and can flee my responsibilities like Jonah). But

at the same time, there is nothing other than the world, nothing beyond it, or only *the* nothing. Writing says, each time,
there is (nothing else, more, or *beyond).* An Orphic glance
can detach from the thing of the world its predicates, its knowability, its features and distinguishing marks, its history and
its form—none of which are other than it and all of which
touch upon its *ipseity.* And it is there, in this detachment, "beside itself," as an originary image, that the thing takes place.
Art "shows" this. The detachment is its "each time"—a singular, articulated instant, a fatal and dying instant unable to
give itself its end. Writing gives this to us *as such;* but we cannot grasp this "gift," for it is no-thing-like. It is how it is. By
the same token, the being of writing itself is "beside itself" in
poetry.

Existence (or Being) takes place in poetry, not in the world
(where it is disseminated in things), because poetry is without
a world and without existents (or beings). But there is nothing
other than the world. Language is the saying of this fatality. It
returns existence to "itself" (never having left itself) just as, at
the end of its itinerary, the temple (the Work) returns to itself—to that which it already no longer was. This is its pure
exposure to irreparability, as Giorgio Agamben would say and
as we shall discuss in our next chapter. The secret of its obsolescence is this "already no longer" that describes its origin.
Already no longer a thing, neither meant nor shown, its being
is its being-toward-itself, toward its death, that at each instant arrests its being-toward, like the superfluity of an instant that must endure its no longer having time. This is likewise the essence of Heideggerian finitude: at each instant one
has already run out of time and *death is possible* (but there is
no longer any time during which or in which to die, as Blanchot
inflects it). The uncanny presence or persistence of the corpse,
or the work of art, realizes this enigma.

Writing, then, exposes or "exscribes"[16] a certain resistant materiality of which we can only say "there is." When we speak of *ipseity* or origin, as we do above, we are indicating an absolute past, immemorially past (since it was never present), and its only "life" is in its persistence in the image of the things of the world, but without its properly "belonging" to the world and the world's personal forms. The temple that returns to its origin, to its materiality, *to itself*, also disappears into itself and becomes its own unnamable image, reckless and ungraspable. *I cannot touch the earth, for I am it, in an uncontrollable identification whose intimacy is its dispersion.* The artist cannot reach materiality, for materiality excludes authority. The very life of materiality is its uncanny persistence in the work of art (or the corpse) and its disappearance into things that rest in the horizons of the world. Thus we must not envision an independent, glorious, and pure pre-predicative life. We must think some "it" that remains always, as it were, "between languages." Unsaid each time, its life is only its translatability, its exposure to being said. It is made up solely of versions. Its life is in that vibration which makes it sensational and leaves it always at the tip of my tongue. Agamben defines it as "purely linguistic existence" and one that, always slipping from my tongue, remains strictly unformulaic, but is eminently reformulaic (and whose only life *is* its reformulations, or its traces, as Derrida and Levinas would say.)

In this way we come very close to the old problem of schematism from Kant's *Critique of Pure Reason* and to the mysterious "art concealed in the depths of the human soul."[17] Recall that the schema provides an image for a concept and that the formation of the schema is called schematism. Now, a schema is not an image and schematism is not imagination, but they are happily related. The schema "shares" with the image some characteristic, but this shared characteristic has *its own nature*. It is neither a simple aspect (a "this here") nor a reproduction (of an absent "this here"). The shared characteristic is called, by Heidegger, in default of a proper name of its own, a *schema-image*.[18] The schema-image is the image of a concept, an image of thought, and it is that by virtue of which a particular can no longer be just anything at all, and becomes instead one among many like it. This is the essence of human intelligence: the subsumption of particulars under universals. By means of the schema-image, the particular becomes, in short, an "example of . . ." Importantly, in becoming an example, the particular relinquishes its prelinguistic indetermination and acquires *all* it determinations because, as an example, *it need not appear as in fact it actually does appear.* This liberation from actuality is *necessary* for it to be subsumed under the universal. As an example, it is *necessarily contingent* (that is, it must be able to appear otherwise than in fact it does appear or it could not be recognized as what it is). There is, then, no *actual* schema-image. The schema-image is a *possible* presentation of the "rule" of presentation represented by the schema. It is an anterior profile into such a thing (but there is no such thing) as a general form of something, for example, a house-in-general. The schema-image is a representation *(Vorstellung)* that must precede any actual presentation. This is the "art" hidden deep in our souls. It is the "production" of that which is, as William J. Richardson says, "not thematized at all,"[19] or of that which is, Agamben will say, neither universal nor particular.[20] The schema-image is a *potentia*, or, as Agamben says, a "halo."[21] It is the particular *with all its predicates*, no one of which or no combination of which, however, distinguishes it as what it is. It is not, Heidegger reminds us, a description that enumerates a list of characteristics. The mind does not work from an imaginary inventory. No particular thing can claim to be the only possible example. We will return to Kantian schematism when, in our next chapter, we discuss Agamben's politics. We bring it up now to indicate the radical direction and orientation of Blanchotian thought toward the "elemental depths," and the icy image that precedes the real and that the real sinks back into in the artwork, the poem, the *récit*.

We can see here that the source of any determinate image, object, or for that matter, any history or narrative (any "this here" or any absent "this here"), is a "rule-image" that is not bound to any definitive representation. The rule-image is imperceptible and it vanishes into its "work" of free construction *(Freibilden)*. It is absent/present *in* any definitive actuality or image exposing that item to *all* its possibilities, and it is nothing other than this empty totality that remains empty because it is never actualized or envisioned. It is, in the words of Agamben once more, *the pure being-in-language of the non-linguistic (l'essere-nel-linguaggio del nonlinguistico)*.[22] Neither an aspect nor a reproduction, this endlessly proliferating "depth's" only essence is its existence in reformulations—being named but remaining silent, outside the text "in" the text. This means that its life is *only* extended and its end is *only* postponed or reprieved as it is each time (re)said. This is why the anonymous narrator of *L'arrêt de mort* insists that "the truth will be told, everything of importance will be told. But not everything has happened yet [la vérité sera dite, tout ce qui s'est passé d'important sera dit. Mais tout ne s'est pas encore passé]," because "[i]t may be that all these words are a curtain behind which what happened will never stop happening [Il se peut que tous ces mots soient un rideau derrière lequel ce qui s'est joué ne cessera plus de se jouer]."[23]

Proximity

The chance of regarding the world, or another person, from the impossible perspective of an infinite distance, or a glacial remoteness, is at the heart of Blanchot's *récits* and his writings on aesthetics, and it is also the kernel of Levinas's *éthique* (which we might just as well grow accustomed to calling "imaginary" in Blanchot's sense, because it is an ethics that resists personal and familiar form). In fact, to follow up on the remarks we made on Levinas in our second chapter, we may keep in mind as we read Blanchot that the aesthetic distance or Orphic glance that so obsesses Blanchot's narrators is, in Levinas's text, identified as an infinite responsibility, or even an uncontrollable compulsion to be for-the-other, which can never be satisfied or used up. This responsibility opens onto a time beyond "my death" that the Other *(Autrui)* "presents" in a *visage* (or an aspect, or image, in the Blanchotian sense) that escapes comprehension and perception just as does the "materiality" of which we speak in the first section of this chapter. Furthermore, this time beyond "my death," or this time that is *en deçà du temps* (the time of the "already no longer"), from which *Autrui* incessantly emerges as *visage*, is also the time of "substitution" or *complete* being-for-the-other that figures as Levinas's most striking and most difficult notion.

This infinite distance or glacial remoteness is also an extreme closeness, contact, or *proximity* in the sense developed at length by Levinas in his *Autrement qu'être ou au-delà de l'essence.* It "lives" in consciousness as a *trace* or a persistent *thought* that cannot be thematized and that haunts the narrator in the second division of *L'arrêt de mort.* The oxymoronic conjunction or disjunction of these two moments—closeness and distance—is intended to indicate a heteronomy, or, if you prefer, a hypocritical schema that is, we may say, too "weak"

to be resolved in simple images or announced in themes. Using Blanchotian language, we can say that proximity *neutralizes* space by neutralizing the fixity of presence. As it will be
spoken of here, proximity is foreign to (or is not identifiable
in) images or thought. (The strategic function of the oxymoron in all of Blanchot and Levinas—not to mention Bataille,
Nancy, Lacoue-Labarthe, and even, sometimes, Heidegger—
is precisely to fatigue and freeze thought into a suspension *en
deçà* dialectics. The "logic" of the oxymoron is the logic of
the Blanchotian image, which, detaching the things of the world
from their involvement in the world, exposes them to "themselves" prior to their mundane investments. The oxymoron
indicates a schema-image—a term that is, of course, itself
oxymoronic—or an "image" of thought that neutralizes that
thought's thinkability. The oxymoron is an image of what remains when a thought—or an image—cannot be absorbed into
discourse. The oxymoron is a hypocritical schema that detaches thought from its power to comprehend.)

Now, the distance referred to here is not the distance consciousness takes from itself in the power of its for-itselfness by
which it maintains itself in its freedom and autonomy, as Hegel
teaches. The distance referred to here is *repulsive*: it is the
distance consciousness takes from what is *never* itself, from
what can be described as absolute vicariousness and from
whose an-archic kiss the ego is expelled into itself in a proximity that cannot become transparent to consciousness. Proximity is a surplus beyond consciousness's ability to thematize;
it is a consciousness that is always "lost," forgetful of itself, or
trapped in a delay behind itself, as Levinas says, because it
cannot bring into the present in a *Vorstellung* (a "placing before") that which affects it.[24] It "forgets" to bring that which
affects it into a present because it has no memory of it. Because of this rendezvous *en deçà* the present, consciousness

never returns altogether to itself. In a formulation that will not surprise psychoanalysis, consciousness (the ego) is not entirely familiar to itself because it "includes" in it an alterity it never intended.

The infected consciousness is not the *I* that magisterially distances itself from the world or from another person. The Blanchotian narrator is not a player in a game of relations. He (always "he," *il*, or "it," always, even to the narrator, "the narrator") is instead involved in a separation of time from time and space from space that opens onto writing because writing is the very approach of obscurity. As *I* write, *he (il)* distances himself while remaining near, unable to annex the space of a present from which or in which to write. *I* cannot write without this affirmation of distancing that does not belong to this time and this place in which I write. But this is also the formula for egoist enjoyment—the enjoyment of a certain holiday from the self.

For example, one day I may return home with a strange desire to move to another apartment and, after a few weeks, I may do just that. But then I may wish to move to yet another apartment, and then yet another, and another, and so on and so on—until I am no longer able to "return" "home." I may even, like the narrator in *L'arrêt de mort*, maintain three or four flats at the same time.[25] What can compel someone to maintain several apartments at once, since he or she cannot inhabit them all simultaneously?

I may give in to this mad impulse because in any one of my apartments I could enjoy my absence from it as well, and at the same time. That is, I could enjoy the fact that I need not sleep here where I am in fact actually lying down for the night. I could get up, dress, and remove myself to any one of my other flats. Each of these others (and there need not be anything special about them) simultaneously houses my absence, sheltering, for as long as I can afford them, another, slightly different, version of this one that I am in. Each one of them says to me: Come. This would be very pleasant. Now and then, I may even ignore all of my flats and rent out a hotel room for a night or two. Or I may spend an entire night wandering the streets without sleeping anywhere, passing, sometimes, in front of one of my apartments where I will have left on the light and the television set in order to savor all the more the possibility of being there. You see, I would belong in any one apartment only by virtue of belonging in each of the others. (Is this not the pleasure bigamists seek out and enjoy?) Each of these various flats would house an anticipation of me and would welcome me inside. No doubt, the narrator of *L'arrêt de mort* sought out and enjoyed this pleasure born of indecision, and even jealously guarded it. (When, in his absence, a little girl stares into a room he rents in a house where others are already living, the narrator becomes furious. He is furious because, gazing at his absence, she takes his place and her gaze precedes and inhabits his room, contaminating his own presence/absence.)[26]

By virtue of remaining pleased with the possibility of fleeing from flat to flat, the narrator finds himself implicated in a world of flats and in vain would he seek out the precise moment he became so implicated. By virtue of taking pleasure in the possibility of his flight from room to room, the narrator encloses himself in himself and he enjoys the separation of subjectivity. The enjoyment is precisely that each "here" is also an "elsewhere." It is not the presence of this room in its actual particularity that contents him, but his savoring of its proximity to each other room he rents out. That which he enjoys is not present, is not consumed or used up, not even partially. This is the only way the flat he is in can truly "materialize." *This* apartment is enjoyable only insofar as it is exemplary of any of his other apartments. Any *this* apartment is, if you like, the schema-image of all the others and it is enjoyable only insofar as it "touches" all of them. Sleeping tonight so contentedly in this flat, he is simultaneously embraced by all the others. Separated from its particularity—from its individual, identifiable existence at this or that address in the city—it does not then become insipidly ideal or universal. Instead, its "life," its "materiality," is only in its proximity. Neither particular nor universal, it is already no longer an object of consciousness. This kind of pleasure departs from any cognitive relation the narrator maintains with any particular flat. The narrator is in any one room only via a distance from/contact with all the others he rents out. He is in this room that is *this* room only by virtue of its similarities to/differences from all the others. This room "includes" the others in it, and in this room, he is the echo of himself in any of the other rooms. In this room, as Levinas says, the ego is "like the echo of a sound that would precede the resonance of this sound [comme l'écho d'un son, qui précéderait la résonnance de ce son]."[27]

The *I* who signs all the rental agreements and the checks to pay for these flats every month is excluded from the pleasure of egoism. The subject can savor this immense pleasure, but only from an immense distance, as if, as Blanchot says, it were separated by a plate of glass from what it nevertheless enjoys, for it can only have a degraded image or conception of that which it enjoys. The *I* is excluded from proximity and egoist enjoyment in which it is nevertheless implicated, but only at a glacial remove because that which the ego enjoys, is touched by, is *in*, remains inconceivable to intentional consciousness. That which is desired, sought out, and enjoyed proximally—in short the place of *jouissance*—is precisely *the divergence of the particular from the universal*. Or, the divergence of the image from the concept. It is a divergence that each time is singular and exclusive. Unperceived, unintended, accidental, erroneous, this divergence is the very incarnation of the materiality of matter. This room that the narrator enjoys *is* only insofar as it is "beside itself," touching all its possibilities.

Such enjoyment is not at all an elevated feeling or a special sensitivity to some quality or aspect of this flat in its particularity. The narrator cannot identify or conceive of what is enjoyed. The enjoyment, in fact, is perfectly negligible. It has no dignity. That is why this egoism is supported or recognized by the subject only as a shadow, an unfamiliarity "too close," or a proximity that overwhelms self-presence. The egoism of this pleasure is "in-itself," is singular and anonymous, and it remains "in itself" insofar as it is without self-recognition, without a pleat of reflection, and is repulsive to intentionality. (The narrator's fury at the little girl who spies on him in his absence is directed to the fact that she "saw" him when he was "not himself," when he was not *there*, just as if she had seen his very egoist pleasure—which he himself is forbidden to "see." What the little voyeur saw, in fact, was a moment of extreme intimacy, which the narrator can only convey to the girl's mother in conventional and banal terms: he said that she had spied on him when he was in his room with a woman. But it was in fact the presence of his absence that he was "with" and that the little girl seemed to be fascinated by.)

To be perfectly perverse about it, all of "these things" that "happened to [the narrator] in 1938 [ces événements me sont arrivés en 1938]"[28] are perfectly negligible, unworthy of commentary, of narration. The narrator does not comment on events of serious public and historic consequence that occurred at around this date and that "occupied [the narrator's] attention all the time [m'ont occupé tous les jours],"[29] because those events, he tells us, are "rotting away, their story is dead, and the hours and the life which were then [his] are dead too [pourissent, leur histoire est morte, et mortes aussi ces heurs et cette vie qui alors ont été les miennes]."[30] He recounts instead events that, we must presume, are not (yet) dead and that did not occupy his attention at the time. The things he recounts do not belong to "the still pleasant shadow of yesterday's world [l'ombre du mond d'hier plaît encore],"[31] but instead are things that are not limited to the past and that continue to attract him even as he attempts "to put an end to it all [mettre fin à tout cela]" in writing the *récit*.[32]

What the narrator recounts, and would like to end, are those things that distracted him: his seeing someone again whom he had forgotten even existed, his multiple dwellings, the strange and unpredictable fluctuations in his (always precarious) health and moods (neither of which he takes very seriously), odd encounters with neighbors, comings and goings in and out of rooms he and others enter by mistake, and his relations with two women (J. and Nathalie) neither of whom he has any intention of marrying (even though he proposes to one of them). None of these things had anything to do with his important and consequential work as a journalist at the time of the Munich crisis. These things he recounts are sometimes immensely pleasurable, sometimes annoying, sometimes grave, and if he is now (after eight years and numerous attempts) able to write of them, it is because he sees that they concern only himself.[33]

While the events of the war years are dead, these inconsequential happenings have managed to live on and remain undead and unrecorded by virtue of their insignificance. By virtue of their insignificance, they escape historical scrutiny and worm their way lackadaisically into the time of his writing. But they are not important to write about now, either. They are what the journalist did not write about at the time because they were inessential events, of secondary importance, mere everyday life. They were already supplementary to the time of the coming war. Unlike the Munich crisis, seeing Simone again after he had forgotten she even existed is a mere trifle— it happened when nothing much else was happening. But in a certain sense, these everyday events are purely historic. They are history purged of historic events, or, the everyday *as* the pure possibility of history. Importantly, for the purpose of approaching Blanchot's aesthetics, we must recognize that these everyday events *already possess the characteristics of writing and of the image.* They are of secondary, inessential, non-primary importance, thus they already open the space of writing. They are what happens when nothing happens, just as writing only happens when nothing happens. The events that he writes of, and wishes to be rid of, are, from the first, *secondary.* They relate to nothing of primary importance. If he did not date the *récit* for us and mention the Munich crisis, would we know that the time frame of the narrative is the eve of World War Two? The "things" the narrator writes of were, from the outset, "traces" in the sense made so well known by Derrida and Levinas.

In his essay "La réalité et son ombre," Levinas tells us that life solicits the novelist when it appears to take the form of a novel.[34] (We need only recall the narrator from *À la Recherche du Temps Perdu,* who is astonished to read a newspaper account of a murder that seems to him to be torn from the pages of Dostoyevsky. He then comes to the realization that, of course, Dostoyevsky's inspiration was precisely the same: a newspaper account of a murder that seemed to be torn from the pages of a novel that he would then sit down to write.)[35] Blanchot, however, never, not even in his essays, writes at the level of form. He writes fragments, and he even writes fragmentarily about fragmentary writing. It is not form that solicits his narrators. A more obscure demand solicits his attention. Anamorphic, the fragment's only life is its separation from any whole, any narrative, any history. It cannot be put in place and therefore demands from the writer something other than form. It demands destruction. It demands, as we say at the outset of this chapter, that *writing tear itself apart from the moment it begins to speak*:

> Writing is not destined to leave traces, but to erase, by traces, all traces, to disappear in the fragmentary space of writing more definitively than one disappears in the tomb, or again, to destroy, to destroy invisibly, without the uproar of destruction.

> [Écrire n'est pas destiné à laisser des traces, mais à effacer, par les traces, toutes traces, à disparaître dans l'espace fragmentaire de l'écriture, plus définitivement que dans la tombe on ne disparaît, ou encore à détruire, détruire invisiblement, sans le vacarme de la destruction.][36]

All the "things" that "happen" in *L'arrêt de mort* are fragments, pieces of no wholes, separations in defiance of presences. That is what gives this and his other *récits* their peculiar atmosphere, their "new thrill [frisson nouveau]," as Levinas says of them.[37] Someone enters by mistake into another person's room and this has untold consequences because nothing about it, or the turmoil it causes, adds up to anything consequential. Nothing of what the narrator desperately wants to say and be rid of will resolve itself into images, thought, commentary, scenes, narrative, or, to sum it up, *text*. Nothing of what he wants to say can be properly reflected. In the end, that which he wants (the truth, of course), he says, "is not contained in these facts. I can imagine suppressing these particular ones.

But if they did not happen, or others happened in their place, and answering the summons of the all powerful affirmation which is united with me, they take on the same meaning and the story is the same [n'est pas dans ces faits. Les faits eux-mêmes, je puis rêver de les supprimer. Mais, s'ils n'ont pas eu lieu, d'autres, à leur place, arrivent et, à l'appel de l'affirmation toute-puissante qui est unie à moi, ils prennent le même sens et l'histoire est la même]."[38] That is why *L'arrêt de mort* is not a masterful attempt to recollect facts and images that at the time *seemed* negligible but that now help us to envision 1938 more richly and more accurately. *L'arrêt de mort* is not a re-counting at all. The *récit* gives us a *un frisson nouveau* because it is curiously and uncomfortably *alive*.

If the narrator is able to suppress certain facts and allow others to replace them it is because he writes without any final or authentic judgment. Either this fact or that one can "tell" the story and the story will remain "the same" because "what happened" is autonymic. It is precisely the resistance to determinate form. The narrator struggles against, and also unites with, this anamorphia as if summoned. We are told, in a postscript (or a surplus that was present at the end of the 1948 version of the text, deleted in the second edition in 1971, and then reattached for Lydia Davis's beautiful English translation in 1978) that if we can "imagine" the hand that writes the story then reading will become for us "a serious task."[39] Serious because the hand that writes the sentences is dead, absent. More absent even than the entombed Lazarus (as Blanchot writes elsewhere)[40] whom we can only imagine as living and not as he really is.

L'arrêt de mort does not await readerly interpretation. It does not preserve or entomb a discourse the reader is obliged to liberate. It is itself the very space of divergence. Most banally, it is the divergence of reader and writer. In a sense, however, both reader and writer are on the same side, while diverging from both of them is the writing, as Steven Shaviro has noted.[41] Each of the incidents written of in *L'arrêt de mort*—J.'s death, return to life, and "second" death; the bombing of Paris and the narrator's taking shelter with Nathalie and proposing marriage to her in a frenzied and foreign language; the return of Simone—each of these incidents is outside the others and each is memorable only insofar as each detaches itself from any time frame. The things written about in this *récit* will not form a narrative. Each incident is an interruption of something else. In this sense they dispense with the author and push him to the same side as the reader whose inability to connect the events told of echo the author's own impotence. Hence, *L'arrêt de mort* is not a Work. It is, as Blanchot puts it, *désœuvrement.* It is *un*worked, idle, and in this regard Blanchot's aesthetics squares perfectly with Levinas's analysis of art. *L'arrêt de mort* is work-less. It is an imitation of thought, a semblance of being, and it is written in a simulated language (i.e., a language that does not communicate but that simultaneously shows and conceals; words appear on the page only to sink back into their own image, so that the difference between being and appearing is erased).

The text we study here does not preserve anything. It is intended to be destructive: "to erase, by traces, all traces."[42] We will not be able to conceive of what "thrills" us as we read Blanchot. His *récit* is not what used to be called a "plural" text. It does not offer itself to a variety of readings, no one of which would be authentic and decidable, leaving the reader adrift in playfulness.[43] Instead, the text "performs" its own disappearance. It "puts an end to it all" in writing, but by putting the end in writing it remains without an end the narrator could put behind him and limit to the past. The *récit* thus disappears by seeking *another* end—an end yet to come in a time not-yet. *L'arrêt de mort* is the "place" of the absence of a proper end, and it holds this place like an echo that precedes the sound it resounds. That is to say, in reading the Blanchotian *récit*, we hear the reverberation of a sound not yet heard, from a time beyond "my death." The text is already an echo of a sound (a speaking, a writing) to come, but that will never be present because it will itself echo the echo the text already is. Not a plural text, *L'arrêt de mort* is a text emptied of all presence and, what is more, it violently empties time of all presence. Put more simply and more abruptly, *L'arrêt de mort* destroys time. The past—the things that happened to the narrator in 1938—are not offered to the reader, to the present, but instead offered to a futurity whose coming our reading already echoes. The *récit* is absolutely indifferent to "my time," "my death." It skips over the present moment.

That which "thrills" us then, when we read Blanchot, is the divergence and disjunction of past and future. Past and future are unhinged because there is no present to insure continuity. (It is, in its way, profoundly political literature. The evacuation of the present renders the future truly futural— i.e., a radically uncertain, but already too near, futurity.) The thrill is the thrill of proximity. The text I read is withdrawn from my presence. It is, as it were, behind glass: too close and also glacially indifferent to me, to my time. As I read, I experience the time of the absence of time, time without a present. Eternally caressed by futurity, this time will never (have) enter(ed) the present because it will always have remained *en deçà du temps*.

The fragments the text records do not—let us be clear about this—await a time to come in which they will be sewn into a Whole, a Work. *L'arrêt de mort* does not await its welcome into a community, culture, civilization, or even a literature. The indifference the text shows to the present tells us that the time it awaits is the time of the forgetting of time, of indifference to time. It is in this sense that the Blanchotian text is so extraordinarily radical. His writing addresses a time outside initiative. But this time to come—a time when time is forgotten—is not a chronological epoch after my death. The time awaited is always happening in everyday events that fragment and separate themselves from a Whole, like the events of *L'arrêt de mort* that "could have happened at a much earlier time [car tout a pu remonter à un moment bien plus ancien]."[44] To await this time is to await forgetting *(l'attente l'oubli)* as Blanchot so succinctly put it in one of his many remarkable titles. But forgetting is not a punctual event. It does not properly arrive at all. Having no duration, it is over before it begins, and it closes in on itself and separates itself from time as a chronological flow. Forgetting defects from time and from initiative. When the time of forgetting comes it will simultaneously have been forgotten and so too will have been forgotten its anticipation.

Let us note that in addition to a thrill, *L'arrêt de mort* is also the site of extraordinary struggles: J.'s struggle against death, the narrator's struggle to write the text after several attempts, his struggle with and against the "thought" to which he gives "all [his] strength [toute ma force],"[45] and his struggle to maintain a relationship with a woman of whom, he says, very seriously, "I can say that by getting involved with Nathalie I was hardly getting involved with anyone [je ne me liais presque avec personne] ."[46] But let us also note the narrator's curious inability to determine the facts that would properly represent these struggles. We have already discussed the anamorphia of the "story." Let us now consider this in light of the narrator's worldly involvements.

In a certain sense, the narrator seems cold and indifferent to his role as the narrator who would judiciously select those details and that language which can fully appreciate the valiance of J.'s fight to live, as well as the relation between the events he recites and the times in which they occur (i.e., the eve of the war that no doubt affected them all, not to mention all the world outside the small circle of characters we read of in this *récit*). Nor does the narrator take the time to explain what the first section of the *récit* has to do with the second. Further, the narrator seems indifferent to his own health and, when he writes of J.'s final hours and her extraordinary courage, he retains a certain journalistic aloofness that is, at the very least, disarming.

All this, in fact, is an effect of anamorphia. What we read here is not a whole. It is not a story *of* J's courage, the war, his life, or anything else. The entire *récit* remains at the threshold of a story. The narrator stops short of presenting some *It* that the story would be about. All that he writes is just anterior to the story, just *en deçà* the story. And yet he tells us everything, as he promises to do on the opening page. He tells us everything because everything is outside the story. Nothing of what he wanted to say was ever properly formed. It was sudden, accidental and moving because it was unprepared-for, unfulfilled, and failed. And it is precisely the failure of the story and the weakness of language to say it that continually exposes him to it, to these unprepared-for events that altered him beyond comprehension. When Blanchot writes on Kafka, he mentions Kafka's lifelong self-recriminations, his ethical crises, his confessions of failure, and his chronic indecisiveness.[47] Blanchot points out, however, that it is possible to flee one's responsibilities by fleeing *into* the world, into one's role as a man of the world: diplomat, bureaucrat, journalist, university professor, or husband. Even those who most zealously and energetically pursue noble political and ethical ends can "hide" like Jonah. But Kafka's indecisiveness and failure were necessary for him to write and to remain face-to-face with his responsibilities, which he saw clearly. To write was to live with his torment and to affirm it to the point of laughter, just as the narrator of L'arrêt de mort lives with and loves the "thought" that "lives and acts like a person even if it isn't exactly like one [n'est pas tout à fait une personne, même si elle agit et vit comme elle]."[48]

At the end of the récit, Nathalie tears apart the pretenses she and the narrator lived under in the delirious days that followed the insincere promise of marriage he made to her in the Metro as Paris was bombed. During that time, the narrator was strongly moved by great emotion and affection for Nathalie. He felt a "limitless impatience to spend time [impatience sans limite d'un temps commun]" with her and he is certain she felt an extreme attraction to him as well.[49] But of that passion he asks:

> —what does it mean? And the word ecstasy? Who has experienced the most intense feeling? Only I have, and I know that it is the most glacial of all, because it has triumphed over an immense defeat, and is even now triumphing over it, and at each instant, and always, so that time no longer exists for it.

> [quel est son sens? Et le mot délire? Qui connaît le sentiment le plus grand? Moi seul, et je sais qu'il est le plus glacé, car il a triomphé d'une immense défaite, et maintenant encore il en triomphe et à chaque instant et toujours, de sorte que pour lui il n'y a plus de temps.][50]

The narrator felt moved to live with Nathalie, but she definitively disrupted his enthusiasm and "wanted to tear apart with a zealous hand the pretenses [they] were living under [n'ait rien voulu de plus que déchirer, d'une main jalouse, les apparences dans lesquelles nous vivons]," and recall him to his "place [lieu]."[51] She then has a plaster cast of her head and hands made for him. That is to say, she offers him her eternal death, a gift (as Levinas's analysis of death shows) that she herself will never experience, will never cross over into. She offers him as his "place" the time of her dying and its glaciality, which is always the most passionate feeling of all since it excludes the one-who-dies from it. She offers him a time in which she is already removed from the world. If the Blanchotian narrator comes across to us as aloof and detached it is because he is no longer himself. The narrator is affected by another time in which he is absent, as we shall see more definitively in our next section.

To write of these things is to remain at the threshold of the world and to live without form—in the absence of the Book, as Blanchot puts it. It is to remain at the threshold of language, of communication. Not at all a refusal of responsibility, writing unites with it, refusing to flee its exorbitance. Writing is the imitation of thought, the simulation of action, and the continual exposure to responsibility, that is to say, to the Other. Writing *is* Blanchot's ethics and his politics. It is formless writing, however. It is radically ambiguous and it unites with this ambiguity. Try to summarize Blanchot's essays. Take *L'espace littéraire* for example. The title of the book and the essays in it could hardly be broader in scope and more inconclusive, verging on interpretation but without "producing" a "reading." But this is precisely the struggle against the Book, the refusal of the present. It is a struggle that takes place as a meticulous indifference to a given community. Emptied of all determinate contents, Blanchot's workless works are already the presentation of a time to come, a book to come *(le livre à venir),* when time is no longer anchored in the present, in continuity. This time will have been atopic. When withdrawal into the world will have been forgotten, one's relation to place, to rootedness, or to home will have been ruptured by the hypocritical continuity of proximity that neither unites into a whole nor scatters into distinct parts, but instead exposes one to all the others such that any one is an echo of each, and none is original.

But is this not just another role *in* the world? How is it not just another version of the poet as conscience of his times? A conscience without contents, if you like, or contentlessness *as* conscience, or as the pure possibility of conscience (or even— why not?—*Gewissen-haben-wollen*), but a conscience nonetheless, and thus assigning the poet a role in given society whether or not he or she likes it. Perhaps this is the case, but there is no room in the world for him or her who, writing, refuses the world. Nor is there any room outside the world. Hence, there is writing, which is neither/nor. Neither conscience nor its lack.

En deçà du temps

The time of the "meanwhile" *(l'entretemps),* which we brought out in our discussion of Levinas's aesthetics and ethics, is of obsessive importance to Blanchot's meditations on art and community. The time of the "meanwhile" is the time "preserved" in the work of art (Levinas), the time of writing and the time of dying (Blanchot), and also, we think, the time of *la comunità che viene* (Agamben). In his discussion of Tiananmen, Agamben observes that the demonstrators made few concrete demands of the government and these were readily granted.[52] He points out that the students did not act in open confrontation to, or competition with, the state over recognizable issues. Instead, Agamben says: "*The nov-elty of the coming politics is that it will no longer be a struggle for the conquest and control of the State, but a struggle be-tween the State and the non-State (humanity), an insurmount-able disjunction between whatever singularity and the State organization [Poiché il fatto nuovo della politica che viene è che essa non sarà più lotta per la conquista o il controllo dello stato, ma lotta fra lo stato e il non-stato (l'umanità), disgiun-zione incolmabile delle singolarità qualunque e dell'organiz-zazione statale]."*[53] (We will take up Agamben's politics at more length in our next chapter, but we want to say in advance that he seems to be describing a politics without determinate con-tents, and a suspension of political time as it is organized by the State. In this interruption, we glimpse a time *à venir*, be-yond, or, *en deçà* State-time. In Tiananmen Square Agamben glimpsed an image, in Blanchot's sense; an image that, in ef-fect, destroyed State-time, and this is why the demonstration was so massively crushed and yet has continued to haunt the State ever since.)

There is a notion we want to bring out in this section of our study that is essential to Agamben's thought but is antici-pated in many pages of writing by Blanchot. It is the notion of an absolute disjunction. "Preserved" in the work of art (or the icon, as Levinas prefers to call the artwork), there is the time of writing or the time of dying that "does not let itself be situated or affirmed in relation to life [ne se laisse situer ou affirmer dans un rapport de vie]," and that "does not localize itself as an event, nor does it last in the way of a temporal becoming; dying does not last, does not end, and, prolonging itself in death, tears this away from the state of a thing in which it would like to rest peacefully [ne se localise pas dans un événement, ni ne dure à la façon d'un devenir temporel: mourir ne dure pas, ne se termine pas et, se prolongeant dans la mort, arrache celle-ci à l'état de chose où elle voudrait se pacifier]."[54] Even death does not bring an end to dying (which is why all suicides, however beautiful, fail to attain their sought-after finale). That death does not complete the movement of dying disturbs the often too facilely understood notion of human finitude: the equation of death with rest and peace. Far from setting a limit to dying, death magnifies its incompletion, placing it, as it were, under glass. Like the time of writing and of the image, it never achieves the present moment. "It cannot give itself the other shore [ne peut pas se donner l'autre rive],"[55] Levinas says. The time of writing and the time of dying disrupt the continuity of time by disjoining past and future. Radically poignant, l'entretemps is radically uncertain, radically unforeseeable time.

The time of writing and the time of dying are the time of radical divergence of past from future. They are discontinuous time. The time of dying is open to a time that will never have been, since it will not have passed through a present. This time, which is an openness onto a time without a present, is both too remote and too near. Void of duration, this discontinuous time hollows itself out, erases, or exscribes itself. I am not completely sensible or conscious of it. Rather, this discontinuity or radical uncertainty insinuates itself into continuous time and is smuggled into consciousness unawares, just as a skilled seducer can inaugurate a seduction in even the most banal conversation without once betraying his or her intentions. As should be all too obvious, we speak here of something extraordinarily subtle. In fact, this void-time is the very hollowing out of time that makes continuity possible in the first place. It is like an empty speech or an imaginary conversation that precedes all intersubjective relations. Unable as we are to speak of it, it is nevertheless affirmed in all speaking. Void-time is imaginary time. In Levinas it is the time of the *dire* that precedes every *dit* and that is not entirely absorbed into any *dit*. In the work of art, the time of writing resonates, just as the statuesque corpse magnifies the time of dying.

If death is, or if the dead are, absolutely masterful, it is because one sees in it the absence of any place in the world. The dead remain *there*, remain perceptible, yes, but only insofar as they rigorously resist any relation to life, to continuity. They refuse to "depart," as life speaks of them, and the elderly woman we spoke of in our introduction must have had an infinite respect for this resistance her husband manifested. One sees in the dead, as in the work of art, an insurmountable disjunction. One comes face-to-face with *l'entretemps*: a time "without me" and beyond "my death." The rites that surround the dead are intended, like philosophy and criticism, to "skip over" this empty interval and make of death an event *in* life and within the continuity life regards itself as. But nothing could be more fragile than this continuity. For preceding it (and preserved and exhibited in the cadaver) is the parody of continuity that is the time of dying. It is a parody of eternal life. In this sense, our relationship with the cadaver is a parody of intersubjectivity. What is always disturbing about our relation with the dead is that this relation exposes an always prior relation that is never consciously included in our living relations with the other person. Exposed in the corpse is the time of dying that silently inverts our conscious relations. The dead expose a scandalous discontinuity that precedes continuous time. Our relation with the dead necessarily confronts us with discontinuity par excellence: a time without a present, *en deçà du temps*, remaining always at the threshold of living, durational time.

The work of art, likewise, exhibits this "hither side" of time that Levinas says is "intolerable to thought [intolérable à la pensée]."[56] We must not be tempted to think that Levinas and Blanchot have uncovered a new mode of thought, or a new category, or an intuition hitherto unattested to in philosophy. To be sure, all of Levinas's concern with an *autrement qu'être* refers (obliquely) to this *en deçà*, and we must think about his *éthique* in light of this. Likewise, all of Blanchot's enigmas communicate with this "hither side" as well. But neither Levinas (in spite of appearances) nor Blanchot has constructed anything like a *corpus* of thought out of a "discovery." Neither of them make a contribution to arts and letters in any conventional sense, and this makes any reading of them unconventionally difficult as well. In our own writing to this point we have been drawn into the complications of any *explication du texte*. We ourselves sometimes write obliquely and oxymoronically, as do Levinas and Blanchot. The *explication* we intended remains stalled, and is still not part of any properly critical context. In fact, we have been repeatedly *repulsed* by Blanchot's work, unable to bring to light the "space of literature" he describes so well. For no matter where one tries to place Blanchot—with Hegel, with Nietzsche, with Heidegger, Freud, Kafka, or even Levinas—he vanishes.[57] This reader thus is exiled: no longer and not yet explicating, no longer and not yet reading. We experience, in spite of multiple precautions, a remarkable *failure* at the heart of any approach to the Blanchotian *œuvre*. Yet it is in our failure that we "encounter" the work (and this is what will eternally justify Shaviro's reading of Blanchot in terms of affect and metamorphosis).[58] Failure is anamorphic and everyone who fails—at anything—struggles against the myriad of chance, uniting with it like an accomplice one surreptitiously lives with. Failure opens the space of literature because failure has many reasons when only one would suffice.

Still, this is only a partial explanation. To read Blanchot's *récits* or his essays is to have to come repeatedly to extreme points of uncertainty, points where one really does not know what to say and where one is a priori deprived of any means to say anything. These moments of enigma and fragmentation are so numerous in Blanchot's work that we must say they are the very "substance" of it. Uncertainty or ambiguity are points at which an encounter, a reading, a discourse, can begin to take place and where the words that will speak it can truly *begin* to be found because they come from nowhere. They come from the ambiguity of an imperceptible metamorphosis such that having nothing to say and no means to say it *itself* begins a discourse. This is what "happens" in Blanchot because all his texts are Sirenic, in the sense he himself describes in his essay on the famous episode from Homer. So alluring, Blanchot's texts remain ambiguous, void of content, hesitant, and of an uncertain status (are they poetic? philosophic? critical?). One can approach them, to be sure, in the manner of Ulysses, by strapping oneself to the sturdy mast of Hegel, Heidegger, Kojève, or whomever. One can also spare others any perception of him at all by not teaching him (because he is "unteachable"). He *is* a "difficult" writer. Quite. For, what Blanchot reveals in his texts is the very attractiveness of literature *as such*, art and writing *as such*, thought *as such*. Who can resist this allure? Who would not, like Orpheus in Hell, want to enter the space of literature and wrest from it the form and figure of that which has so affected one? It is not literature, philosophy, or literary criticism that Blanchot writes, but *their infinite attractiveness*. Not literature, but its *image*; not a text, but a *récit*; not thought, but its simulacrum. *The Blanchotian text is the shimmering and pure appearance of literature*. It is poetry *as* pure appearance, pure seeming, pure ambiguity. Neither literature nor thought as it is now thought of, but as it is to come, void of presence in a time *à venir*. And so it is futile and fatal to attempt an explication of Blanchot—

yet without the attempt one will never come to the moment of uncertainty that is simultaneously, and not by analogy, the time of dying and *its* extraordinary and stupefying attractiveness. For the corpse, make no mistake, is *attractive par excellence*, even as it repulses.

When the narrator of *L'arrêt de mort*, through the force of his love and desire, brings J. back from the dead, we read that her eyes "opened abruptly and they opened to reveal something terrible which I will not talk about, the most terrible look a living being can receive [brusquement elles s'ouvrirent, et elles s'ouvrirent sur quelque chose de terrible dont je ne parlerai pas, sur le regard le plus terrible qu'un être vivant puisse recevoir]."[59] Like Orpheus, the narrator has gone into Hell to find his beloved and he has looked at her face-to-face. J.'s eyes look at the narrator from death. Eyes that would look at us from death allow us to come face-to-face with death in person. It is of course a commonplace that one close the eyes of the deceased so that they do not cruelly continue to gaze, to search out for something to see; for this dead gaze—purely indifferent, blank, and superfluous—*is a gaze nevertheless*. In the face of the dead and in the work of art (which has its own blankness) one is faced with the eternal, the endless—not death as absent, but death as the absence of another shore and without any place in life. To close the eyelids of the dead is to pretend that the dead sleep in peace. But human eyes do not sleep. Even in sleep they pathetically search behind closed eyelids for something to see. Human eyes and their gaze do not merely, as Sartre teaches, resist my appropriation. They resist any proper relation to life at all. They are already little corpses. The narrator could revive J., but he is powerless to resuscitate her eyes, which are always already "beyond"—from beyond and vainly searching for a beyond.

In the arrested, stupefied gaze of the dead one sees the

image of a gaze. One sees an imaginary seeing. One sees a gaze that is the gaze of no one. (And that is why, in the myth, Euridice vanishes when Orpheus looks at her, or at her gaze—for hers is the gaze of no one, the gaze of the dead.) There is a double opening of J.'s eyes (they "opened abruptly and they opened to reveal [brusquement elles s'ouvrirent, et elles s'ouvrirent sur]"), because there must be a dead, blank, anonymous gaze that hollows itself out and creates a space for seeing. It was that blank gaze that the narrator confronted in J.'s eyes. It was a gaze that resembled J.'s but that *was not hers, was not anyone's*. The eyes that looked like J.'s, for a moment, belonged to no one. At that moment, J. became her own double, her own image, and it was the image of J. that stared at the narrator with an imaginary stare. It was the image of J., yes, but J. herself was abruptly eyeless. The eyes that stared were not hers and it was those anonymous eyes that stared at the narrator as he looked into a face with no eyes: a face he loved and had brought back from Hell.

The image of a gaze preceded J.'s glance at the narrator and J.'s image preceded her return to life. It was an image terrible and unnamable, or an "absent absence," as Foucault puts it.[60] In other words, a resemblance preceded the actual and then disappeared into Hell as J. returned to life. But the living J. (the other subject, to use the crude language of the philosophers) is not the woman the narrator sought, for J., returned to life, returned at the same time to mortality and, in fact, a few days later, the narrator helps her to die.[61] That which preceded J.—her image and its imaginary gaze—was simultaneously her past (herself dead, or "already no more than a statue [déjà plus qu'une statue]," the narrator says)[62] and her future (again, herself dead a few days later). That which preceded J.—the terrible resemblance—was without a present, without being, and bore no relation to the present. In that moment of absolute uncertainty, the Outside was there, death was there—open, impotent, and without intimacy. The narrator was greeted by the gaze he was drawn to and sought for. It was indifferent to him, to his presence, and it condemned him to death because it looked at him *as if he was already no longer there.* Yes, the narrator of *L'arrêt de mort* does find J., the J. he sought, in Hell. But he only meets her who disregards him. He meets her as she *is:* dead and without him, outside him utterly.

The narrator is not aware of this strangeness at the time, for the event is too precise and too impersonal even to be acknowledged. He says, "[I]f I had shuddered at that instant, and if I had been afraid, everything would have been lost, but my tenderness was so great that I didn't even think about the strangeness of what was happening, which certainly seemed to me altogether natural because of that infinite movement which drew me toward her [si à cet instant j'avais frémi, et si j'avais éprouvé de la peur, tout eût été perdu, mais ma tendresse était si grande que je n'eus même pas une pensée pour le caractère singulier de ce qui se passait, qui me parut certainement tout à fait naturel, à cause de ce mouvement infini qui me portait à sa rencontre]."[63] The "infinite movement" he speaks of, the Hell into which J. had slipped, is *l'entretemps:* a crossing that is infinite, arrested, like a (step not) beyond or *le pas au-delà* (as Blanchot so neatly says in the title of another of his works that should perhaps be read as a clandestine companion to *L'arrêt de mort*).

It is important for us to consider the precision of the event for these precise moments make up the "substance" of Blanchot's writings. These moments, or movements, or spaces are precise and anamorphic insofar as they cannot be interrogated, or even properly experienced or narrated. The Outside of which we speak in the scene(s) of J.'s death(s) is not outside of an interiority (the narrator's or the reader's). If we and numerous other commentators so frequently invoke topography, it is only immediately to contest it. *L'entretemps* must be thought of proximally, in the sense we have already discussed. That which happens to the narrator does not, as we see, inspire memorable images or dazzling prose. The tone of *L'arrêt de mort* is, if anything, distant, but with that distance that Blanchot has found at the heart of intimacy and passion. What remains attractive to the narrator is rendered in outline only, in profile only (as is *le visage* in Levinas). Barely perceptible scenes and figures appear (or appear only obliquely, or *appear to appear*) throughout all of Blanchot's works. (*Le pas au-delà* also contains scenes of death, conversations, and "characters" even more sparsely drawn than those in *L'arrêt de mort*.) What "happens" is always "between" (or in parentheses) what might be called actions or events. What matters and what affects us as readers, and what affects Blanchot's narrators in all his *récits*, are events that take place outside any character's initiative or intention. The narrator of *L'arrêt de mort* is able to write and to try to put an end to these events because, he says, they concern only him. Yet that which is only his, that which belongs within his own intimacy, is open to strangers, to readers. Few, if any, works in this century (or ever perhaps) cause the reader to feel more acutely that he or she is *intruding* on someone else's privacy than do the works of Blanchot. This is indeed part of their "thrill." It is as if one had entered a prohibited space or had stepped uninvited into someone else's apartment.

The curious effect here is one of a transgression of intimacy: witnessing that which doesn't concern one. These "things" that happened to someone in 1938 are attractive precisely insofar as they concern only that someone. It is like the thrill of gossip. These things attract me precisely insofar as I cannot relate to them. And if I can "imagine the hand that writes them,"[64] I will only find myself face-to-face with a gaze that does not regard me, that dispenses with me. For that is the "price" of transgression: *I* am neglected. Reading then becomes *une tâche sérieuse* because *l'entretemps* substitutes itself for and simulates—insists on the absence of—the present. To be sure, in all art as we have seen, the "meanwhile" replaces the present, the image substitutes itself for the concept. In Blanchot, this enigma is foregrounded. By "thinning out" images, scenes, characters, actions, and language the Blanchotian text approaches the imaginary *as such*—where there are no images, where nothing crystallizes into definite forms or figures, and where the time of reading is also the time of writing and the time of dying. We reach the shadow of the world where initiative and action are already no longer possible. That is to say, reading comes to double the pathos of dying. It doubles the inability to enter into the present and the impossibility of finding any proper place in the world. It is the time of radical incompletion and of worklessness.

If, as we say, our relation with the dead is a parody of intersubjectivity, it is because it is an imaginary relation: a relation with no one. But it is a relation nonetheless, and one that does not terminate our relations with the one who the dead person was. It is a relation without relation, but it "preserves" and exhibits that vacant time *en deçà du temps* that always precedes the living time of human intersubjectivity. It is parodic in the sense that it is a relation with the other that touches him outside his subjectivity in the time of dying that the other will never come to the end of. It is not a time or a relation that I am ever conscious of in my dealings with others. It is thus a relation over which I can exercise no mastery whatsoever.

The infinite movement toward, or rendezvous with, Levinas's *Autrui* is likewise eternally paralyzed and without an outcome, as is our relation with the artwork. It is, if you like (and as Levinas would prefer), a movement toward an Outside that is only ever rebegun in any conscious undertaking with others in the world. It is a time or a movement "without me," and its intimacy is precisely its disregard of me. The encounter with *Autrui* is emptied both of myself and the other, as if I were obliged, as the "price" of this intimacy, to forget both myself and the other. We have already taken up this issue in our chapter on Levinas. In its intimacy and anonymity, as Blanchot so matchlessly expresses it throughout *L'arrêt de mort*, we must be attentive to that which precedes all living relations and to that which, as it is anonymous, is imaginary. This justifies, we think, our characterization of the Levinasian *éthique* as imaginary.

Immemorially paralyzed, interrupted, hesitant, coy (all these terms will have to do for now) this *en deçà*, or *le dire*, or Image, or Imaginary is just as immemorially forgotten, ignored, overlooked, and dispensed with as inconsequential. In one of his essays on Blanchot, "The Servant and Her Master," Levinas speaks of this "forgetting" as that which restores diachrony to time by turning "away from the past instant [détourne de l'instant passé]."[65] But, importantly, diachrony is not a duration. It has neither "protention nor retention," as Levinas says, good student that he is of Husserl.[66] (When, here and there—in *Autrement qu'être ou au-delà de l'essence* for instance—Levinas speaks of *diachronie*, he means the "meanwhile" that we have been discussing in this chapter.) However, that which turns away from the past also "abides in words [demeure en une parole]"[67] and when they become "attentive to their condition, words come to a stop and turn into pillars of salt [penchés sur leur condition, les mots s'arrêtent en statues de sel]."[68]

Poetry, including the poetry of Blanchot, can "betray itself, become engulfed in order and take on the appearance of a cultural product [se trahir et s'engloutir dans l'ordre pour se montrer produit culturel]" and poetry, of course, can be "applauded and rewarded, sold, bought [applaudi et primé, vendu, acheté]," and so on.[69] This is because, Levinas says, poetry surfaces at a precise instant between knowledge and culture, between seeing and saying.[70] For that very reason, he argues, the two "pincers" are never quite closed—"le moment entre le voir et le dire où les mâchoires restent, entr'ouvertes."[71] The artwork is the resistance to their ever completely closing. Likewise, we think, the relation with *Autrui* that Levinas calls ethics is an obscure resistance to the closing of ontic categories.

The point we are getting to in this chapter is this point of resistance, this interminable paralysis that makes up the "substance" of Blanchot's *œuvre* and is, we may say, the Image of an Outside, and an Other to the categories of thought or of the State. The artwork, the Blanchotian *récit*, Tiananmen, and Levinasian *responsabilité* are discontinuities and disjunctions. Agamben, as we shall see, thoroughly exploits this interminable failure (or, as he will put it, this "power to not not-be [poter non non-essere]")[72] in his writings on the "coming community." What we have tried to bring out of the shadows in our chapter on Blanchot is the sense that the time of continuity and intersubjectivity (as we persist in calling it) is radically undermined and hollowed out by a "forgetting," or a profound "past" *intolérable à la pensée*.

The Image and Ipseity of Art

We have seen that the trajectory of Blanchotian and Levinasian aesthetics is toward anteriority *as such*. Not a primordial state-of-things, nor a fluid and incoherent mass of data awaiting organized impression, but instead the subtlety of imaginary matter (like *le dire* that overflows every *le dit*) whose destiny is neither subjective nor objective. In the disengaged, more-than-passive and otherwise-than-worldly work of art (as in the cadaver), this anteriority is "frozen" and "preserved" as an icon. Yet it remains unperceived and silent, like the *voix narrative*, because it is not the material for a perception. This anteriority *en deçà du temps* is not destined for the light of day, but neither is it the day's simple obverse. In Blanchot's terms, it is the *autre nuit*.[73]

When Blanchot asks of the work of art, "What has always eluded its language [qu'est-ce qui s'est toujours dérobé à son langage]?" and answers, "Itself"; when he says that art "is always anterior to what it speaks of and to itself [est toujours plus antérieur que ce dont il parle et plus antérieur que lui-même],"[74] he is referring to anteriority insofar as art is that which resists its own unveiling and thus eludes the vice-grip of seeing and saying. For, the *voix narrative* is the tale *itself*, the work of art *itself*, prior to its narrative "contents." This is not so very strange. All of the reality of art (like all of the reality of the self, as we have already discussed)[75] is borrowed from outside it: from materials, clay, marble, pigment, and life itself, which sometimes appears to the artist to be already aesthetically attractive. Art is mimesis, according to one of the West's oldest definitions. Art, quite simply, has no self, no *ipse*, to be revealed. That is the secret of its anteriority, its "other night." *Its itselfness is always to come.* This is the secret of its inexhaustible resources. Mimesis cannot be revealed. If the work of art eludes *itself*, and never speaks *itself* in its *own* language, it is because art is precisely selfless. It is without anything that would be proper to it. Prior to its "contents," the work of art is a pure image of itself, an image of nothing. By the most elementary logic we must conclude with Blanchot and Levinas that art *itself*—mimesis—is nothing.

Nothing other than its mimetic rapport with what it is not—
the real. Art is reality's shadow—that which vanishes when
any light is shed on it.

The artwork is not an object. It is pure rapport, pure communication, pure passion. As Blanchot so obligingly puts it:
"It is as if a secret law required of the work that it always be
concealed in what it shows and that it only show what must
remain concealed and that finally it only shows what must
stay hidden by concealing it [Comme si une loi secrète exigeait
d'elle qu'elle soit toujours cachée en ce qu'elle montre, et qu'elle
ne montre aussi que ce qui doit rester caché et ne le montre,
enfin, qu'en le dissimulant]."[76] The work of art "reveals" its
own hiddenness, it "shows" its own absence from all showing, it "says" its own silence, and so forth. Before the work of
art communicates anything (the gods, e.g.) it communicates
communication. It is only *after* that to which the work of art
refers is forgotten (i.e., the gods who have fled and whose
flight too has been forgotten) that this enigma begins to make
itself felt, begins to draw near to its "original experience."
This vanishing point is what Blanchot is getting at when he
asks: "What will become now of art, now that the Gods and
even their absence are gone, and now that men's presence offers
no support [Ne pouvant plus prendre appui sur les dieux, ni
même sur l'absence des dieux; ne pouvant s'appuyer sur l'homme
présent qui ne lui appartient plus { . . . } que va devenir l'œuvre?]"[77]
A fascinating question. It is at this point that the work of art
truly finds its condition, its "elemental depths." It becomes a
pure image of itself, and it disappears into itself, into its time.

Inexhaustibly communicating with what it is not, the work
of art resembles, again, nothing so much as a cadaver whose
very materiality is the erasure of the border between presence
and absence, life and death, disappearance and return, image
and reality (for the cadaver's entire reality is that it is an image

of itself). Like the corpse, the work of art is incapable of its "now," incapable of being itself, incapable of reaching or attaining its being, which always slips beyond it where it cannot step. Like the corpse, the work of art is the very image of a strange incapacity simply to *be*. Like the dear departed, the work of art cannot disappear into its *own* disappearance, its *own* end. This impotence, however, is its "ownmost" experience of "itself." That is, it can only experience "itself" in its other, *as* other. It can only experience itself as other than itself; it *is* only itself as other than itself. It can only communicate, in short. Art is no sooner itself than it is already petrified into a statue, an icon, a puppet, a toy. "She who was once absolutely alive was now no more than a statue [Elle n'était déjà plus qu'une statue, elle absolument vivante]," Blanchot's narrator says of J. at her death.[78] No sooner does she die than she becomes other than herself, *other than anyone*—totally anonymous. Like the cadaver, the work of art *itself* is the image *of an image*. It is an imaginary image, to be sure, and one that nobody recognizes, but it is an image nonetheless and one that is that is always "older" than that of which it is the image. In this way we can understand perhaps more clearly Blanchot's "other version" of the imaginary:

> To experience an event as an image is not to free oneself of that event, to dissociate oneself from it, as asserted by the esthetic version of the image and the serene ideal of classical art, but neither is it to engage oneself with it through a free dimension: it is to let oneself be taken by it, to go from the region of the real, where we hold ourselves at a distance from things the better to use them, to that other region where distance holds us, this distance which is now unliving, unavailable depth, an inappreciable remoteness become

in some sense the sovereign and last power of things.
This movement implies infinite degrees. Thus psychoanalysis says that the image, far from leading us outside of things and making us live in the mode of gratu-
itous fantasy, seems to surrender us profoundly to ourselves. The image is intimate because it makes our intimacy an exterior power that we passively submit to:
outside of us, in the backward motion of the world
that the image provokes, the depth of our passion trails
along, astray and brilliant.

[Vivre un événement en image, ce n'est pas se dégager
de cet événement, s'en désintéresser, comme le vou-
draient le version esthétique de l'image et l'idéal serein
de l'art classique, mais ce n'est non plus s'y engager
par une décision libre: c'est s'y laisser prendre, passer
de la région du réel, où nous nous tenons à distance
des choses pour mieux en disposer, à cette autre région
où la distance nous tient, cette distance qui est alors
profondeur non vivante, indisponible, lointain
inappréciable devenue comme la puissance souveraine
et dernière des choses. Ce mouvement implique des
degrés infinis. La psychanalyse dit ainsi que l'image,
loin de nous laisser hors de cause et de nous faire vivre
sur le mode de la fantaisie gratuite, semble nous livrer
profondément à nous-mêmes, intime est l'image, parce
qu'elle fait de notre intimité une puissance extérieure
que nous subissons passivement: en dehors de nous,
dans le recul du monde qu'elle provoque, traîne, égarée
et brillante, la profondeur de nos passions.][79]

"Older" than the serene classical version of the image that
guarantees distance, is that which is not to be and that which

is not to become either. The work of art is the image of that which is never to be, never to become—that which is ever on the hither side of time *(en deçà du temps)*. *Eternally Mona Lisa will be about to smile.* Eternally delayed prior to being/ becoming, she is the degraded image of the eternal. Not a timeless static form, but a *fragment of a never to be continued and completed whole.* In the corpse, in the work of art, we see (without perceiving) that which images *itself.* It is not another image, as we learn from Blanchot, but another version of the same image. It is a return of the image *to itself*, prior to its being an image of . . . The "other" version of the imaginary is its eternal return to itself, to the same image. No sooner is the artwork finished than it is arrested, other than itself, or, to say the same thing, the "same" as itself in its very alterity. In this arrested time there is no "now" in which the artwork can become. It is the repetition of the real, and repetition is without a present.

Every statue, every cadaver, every puppet, toy, or artifact— indeed, every thing and every person who falls, if only for a moment, outside utility—returns to an inconceivable image void of either subject or object. This is the "last power of things." They invert the "motion of the world" and "return us to ourselves," but to ourselves insofar as there is no one to return to, no society of identities in which we can recognize ourselves. In this "other" imaginary, subject and object disappear as such, as ob-posed and distanced. What remains is pure *-jection* (or thrownness), like Nietzsche's (or Heidegger's) dice.

Art (the tale, the *voix narrative*) is the "forgetting" of subject and object and is in fact their radical identification, fusion, or desegregation. Experiencing the event as an image is an experience in which the object is disavowed as such, as *ob*ject opposed to us in a *Vorstellung* (a "placing before"), and thus it "returns" the subject to itself prior to *its* op-positioning.

In this way, the "experience" Blanchot refers to must be prior to Kantian experience and would refer to the *pure position of the subject*. To experience the event as an image, then, is not to experience an object (since the object disappears into itself), but to experience the self *as* the pure passivity of position, or, "thereness." It is thus prior to any experience of the world, and it immediately closes in on itself without a trace. It closes because the subject can "feel" only its own intrinsically empty receptivity. It is, as it were, the shadow of the receptivity that, uniting with spontaneity, forges the properly Kantian experience. In the language of Levinas, it is an extreme passivity that cannot simply be opposed to activity, because it is the passivity whose only "quality" is infinite receptivity or malleability. It is the passivity of *absolute* instability. That is to say, this experience closes in on itself and leaves no trace because it is never even opened. In absolute passivity, in its pure position prior to any ob- or sub-jection, the "subject" (or shall we say, the "communicatant"?) is what it is not, and is not what it is. There is, quite simply, no containing the essential ambiguity, or the "essential solitude"[80] of communicativity.

The space of literature—or, as we can now say, the space of absolute passivity or communicativity—is the thick, crepuscular, and paroxysmatic materiality of thought that thickens into a "thing" (the "thing" we can say, that the narrator of *L'arrêt de mort* "lives with").[81] It is the erasure of the subject-object hyphen, the erosion of mastery, the erosion of that distance which allows us to hold the world at a distance. For Blanchot, as for Derrida of "before the letter," the name of this movement is writing: the paradoxical "strength" of an inexhaustible impotence. Of this space we can only say that it is . . . , there is . . . , *il y a*. If writing obscures that of which it speaks it is because writing—whose "original experience" art approaches— is the obscurity, or the forgetting, anterior to any memory.

To us, art remains "constantly invisible [constamment invisible],"[82] hidden, *en deçà*, and an *autre nuit*. But we are drawn to it nonetheless. When the object is doubled and neutralized in the image, when the image withdraws the object from the world, and when the object disappears into its own image—then it exercises its fascination, its "powerless power." Writing is the coming of an impotence that neutralizes subjectivity by neutralizing the object. "I," as Blanchot says, become "he" [*il*, the Neuter]. In this doubled space, this shadow of the real, I cease to be sub-ject and become "he" who *is* "his" rapport with that which holds "him" in its spell. For, in the space of literature, I *am* that "he" to whom I eternally return in this timeless time of repetition and incompletion. I am "he" in whom I do not recognize myself. Yet, I am nothing other than "his" return, "his" immemorial and eternal return. And "he" is imaginary—pure passion, pure rapport, pure communication. I am "he" who I am not, for "he" is not (and never will be) who "he" is.

This does not mean that the artwork harbingers my death. It means that an *un*life, an *arrested* death, a paralyzed force, hollows out the time of duration and remains my invisible, hidden involvement with a time of radical incompletion. The artwork does not harbinger death, it *is* my involvement with death already. All of Blanchot's work borders on this "other night" and is carried along in its infinite movement. Not at the end of a worldly itinerary, but at every instant, the time *en deçà du temps* disappears into itself, erases itself, *exscribes* itself. This movement cannot be unveiled, not because it is basically withdrawn and absent, but because it does not belong to the light at all. It is the time of *il*—always already fabricated, fictioned, worked over, and, as such, it is *irrecuperable* time.

Writing, then, is the very movement that forgets "itself,"

erases "itself," for it is without any self. Not simply with-drawn from all presence, this time of writing is, in the lan-guage of Agamben, an *imaginary youth* that *never-has-been* and that re-moves itself each time. It is that whose "self" *is* its re-moval. To sum it up, then, writing—or art, which can double up and preserve every thing that presents itself to us—*is* for-getting. But it is not a forgetting of any *thing*. It is a forgetting that precedes eidetic evidence/a forgetting immemorially for-gotten/not even absent/always already forgotten/a perpetual lack of vision that precedes all seeing and saying/ . . .

Blanchotian aesthetics leads us to, and is constantly in-vaded by, an anteriority incompatible with presence, a "hither side" that is anterior to objectivity. It is the "last power of things" to exercise a silent and forgotten fascination that opens the space of literature, a space evacuated of subject and ob-ject, and thus a space of radical identification and affectivity. The work of art, like the cadaver, before it represents any thing (or scene, or drama, or person), first of all communicates com-munication itself, or being-in-relation. Insofar as I am evacu-ated of subjectivity, I *am* this being-in-relation itself, *my*self. Older than any speculation is this *obsession*. If Blanchot de-scribes this as an "other version" of the imaginary, it is only because there is no word for it. It is not desire, but obses-sion—an *in*-forming that precedes any object or information. It is a dependency that precedes any psyche that would be dependent. There is no subject in this "space" but instead an infinite dependency, malleability, suggestibility, or pure pas-sivity of position that will be ever anterior to any present.

Prior to subject and object—and this is crucial to Levinasian ethics—there is a violent affect, intrusion, or more-than-inti-macy that is invisible, undetectable, ineradicable, and irreduc-ible. It is an "other" beginning outside any origin. It is neuter—

"there is." It is a region in which the Other is not only other than I but also other than he or she. Profoundly unpresentable, this region in-forms me prior to any actual communication or distance. In every image there is already that which I ("I") *am*, my*self*. The writer is he who speaks while *entirely* traversed and transfixed by the *other* that he *is*, the "he" who is never anyone—never anyone other than I, *myself*, but without me.

FOUR

Agamben and the Political Neuter

Anonymity and Belonging

We learn from Blanchot that to write is to pass
from "I" to "He," *il,* the Neuter. The Neuter is the space of
literature (an imaginary space *en deçà du temps*), which is
interminable, incessant, and perpetually noncontemporary. The
neuter is the time of inaction and no initiative. It is the shadow
of time, of the real, of my hand, Blanchot says, as it grips the
pen and writes these words. The writer would like to express
himself with words, but he finds only their shadow, their sheer
appearance, and nothing beyond. The writer, liking it or not,
writes an imaginary language that he cannot put to work and
to which he cannot give life. The writer can "believe he is
asserting himself in language, but what he is asserting is completely without a self [peut croire qu'il s'affirme en ce langage,
mais ce qu'il affirme est tout à fait privé de soi]" and "he can
never again express himself and he cannot appeal to you either, nor let anyone else speak [il ne peut plus jamais s'exprimer
et il ne peut pas davantage en appeler à toi, ni encore donner

115

la parole à autrui]."[1] In the neutralizing space of literature, he loses the power to say "I," and he finds he cannot "give life to characters whose freedom would be guaranteed by his creative force [donner vie à des personnages dont sa force créatrice garantirait la liberté]."[2] To write, to enter the Neuter, "is to arrange language under fascination, and, through language, in language, to remain in contact with the absolute milieu, where the thing becomes an image again, where the image, which had been allusion to a figure, becomes an allusion to what is without figure [. . .] when there is no world yet [c'est disposer le langage sous fascination et, par lui, en lui, demeurer en contact avec le milieu absolu, là où la chose redevient image, où l'image, d'allusion à une figure, devient allusion à ce qui est sans figure et { . . . } quand il n'y a pas encore de monde]."[3]

This obscure region, sketched out in "The Essential Solitude" (and in many, if not all, of Blanchot's other essays) is the region of the *il y a:* "[A]lien to revelation, not even because it is radically dark, but because it transforms everything that has access to it, even light, into anonymous and impersonal being, the Not-true, the Not-real and yet always there [étranger à toute révélation, ni même parce qu'elle serait radicalement obscure, mais parce qu'elle transforme tout ce qui a accéss à elle même la lumière, en l'être anonyme impersonnel, le Non-vrai, le Non-réel et cependant toujours là]."[4] (We should note that this description of Blanchot's could easily have been written by Levinas.) To write is to be "possessed" by anonymity, to be seized by it and infinitesimally retarded. This "milieu" is absolute because it does not refer to any place in the world. It ab-solves itself from the real, and is an absence of inside or outside. To write is to lose oneself in this region where there is nothing to be revealed, expressed, meant, or shown, because nothing is even hidden. It is the region of ambiguity, abandoned by references, emptied of subject and object—where all is such as it is. Irreparably so.

The writer, then, is "possessed" by no one, by the anonymous. He cannot narrate himself, because he is no one; he is *Quelqu'un*, Someone but no one in particular—*das Man*. The Blanchotian writer is not Anna O. who was "possessed" by "another me" such that no exteriorization of this other was ever possible for her in the mode of narrative, as Freud (and Lacan) wished, because she was *herself* the demon who possessed her.[5] Writing is not a case of hysteria. The hysteric is not Homer, who could pass from first to third person, from pure to dramatic diegesis. The discourse of the hysteric, as of any multiple-personality patient, is not a *mixed mode*.[6] To write is not to pass from "I" to another "I." It is to pass from "I" to *il*, to the neutralization of all identities, of all "I's." Writing is not hypnotic or ventriloquized speech. It is not the somnambulistic discourse of someone ravished by another ego.[7] Plato's Ion was not demonically possessed. But Plato saw in Ion the image of madness, an image of radical depropriation. Furthermore, we learn from Philippe Lacoue-Labarthe[8] that Plato "caught a glimpse of" and "reduced to a literary problem" the very "terrorizing" possibility that discourse itself contains, or *is*, the very possibility of a *general* mimesis, a *general* instability that is in fact positive and powerful especially in those fables, or "old wives' tales," that have no author, no guarantor somewhere in the world to answer for their veracity. These "paradoxically authoritative" fables, as Lacoue-Labarthe describes them, are begun in the mode "it is said" and exist, therefore, entirely within discourse itself. They are, in fact, exemplary of all authority. Thus Plato sought to rid discourse of this instability and tendency towards Homericism by targeting poets and making them responsible for the veracity of discourses they only re-cite. In fact, however, discourse *is* this impurity, this hesitation between "I's." Discourse is *neutral* with regard to its propriety. There is a natural ambiguity in discourse with regard to authority, and to speak, or to write, is first to pass to this equivocality. There is no final way, method, or technique that can rid discourse of its essential ambiguity. To write is to pass to this purely linguistic space where I am prior to myself, where speaking is the pure passion of speaking-being itself, depropriated of all identity and near to madness, if not already its image.

To write, or to speak, is to enter into that which, in itself, precedes itself. It is to be stripped of all identity and to become a pure image (of no one)—unable anymore to be, or not to be. It is to become, not another persona, but instead the pure passion of communication, where passion *is* communication and where my identity is this passionate, vertiginous "no one" who cannot answer for what is written. This space is the pure anteriority or pure reserve from which all art comes. It is unlivable, unendurable (i.e., it has no duration) and it is that which withdraws from any actual state of affairs. Writing is a petrified transcendence, an event that is not even potentially accomplishable. It is always "between," or "meanwhile." To pass to *il* is to pass to "he" who carries out an infinite movement ("infinite degrees," Blanchot says).[9] Writing moves us toward that which is always in-itself, that which depends on no condition since it is alien to all actuality, initiative, and accomplishment.

We have seen in previous chapters that the work of art immediately detaches itself from the conditions (the materials and the actual historical states-of-affairs) that it sprang from. We saw as well in *L'arrêt de mort* that, at the instant of her death, J. became no longer herself, no longer any one. At the instant of her death she exhibited that "she" who is quasi-eternally preserved in-herself, always at the lips of the actual without ever attaining it. At the instant of her death, J. no longer depends on all that she was, yet she is none-other than "all that she was." She becomes, in that sense, all that is subtracted from her.

Likewise, the work of art attains a strange independence from all that went into it. It no longer bears any dependence on any real conditions and, from the "start" of its "life" (as an artwork), it separates itself from the world so that it becomes a pure resemblance resembling nothing. It becomes in-itselfness. When I look at a painting or when I read a novel, I perceive without perceiving anything. I am affected without finding myself in any particular state of mind. The work of art, as we have said, is made up of imaginary, fabulous matter that is indistinguishable from the sensations it evokes. Imaginary matter is sensational because it cannot be dissociated from sensation itself (i.e., sensation before it is a sensation *of* something). The work of art is nothing but fabulous, imaginary, sensational matter—matter emptied of the space it would occupy and that, "simple and absolute," hurls itself towards us.[10] Imaginary matter confuses matter and sensation such that sensation becomes exteriority and takes on its own life independent of any *sensum*. In the work of art there is no longer any reference to subject and object, and sensation itself is born in the liberation of matter from objectality. Imaginary matter is incommensurable with objectality and is the very thickening of the hyphen that separates/links subject-object. When matter no longer adheres to an object, it suddenly "appears." But as it "appears" as no object or no form, it immediately disappears. That is, it does not enter into any perception, but rather it begins (or rebegins) an infinite contestation of perception. Levinas has shown us that "painting is a *struggle* with sight."[11] This struggle is the return of the *dynamis* of sensation itself, before sensation enters into any experience (in the Kantian sense). The struggle Levinas refers to is a pure affection—as passive as it is dynamic, as dynamic as it is passionate. Art tends toward this infinite, persistent movement that is the affection of sensation by the imaginary materiality it itself is. Sensation itself, or pure passion, is neutral. It is the exteriority of our most passionate interiority, as we shall discuss more thoroughly later in this chapter.

Our rapport with the artwork, as with the cadaver, is not made up of memories but of the sudden eruption of the immemorial—a rapport that is continually subtracted from all actual, representational states one may have enjoyed with the departed or with that which the artwork prima facie represents. That is to say, we enter into a rapport that is *autonomous* and whose relation to all lived and memorial experiences or states of mind is always equivocal. This rapport, which the artwork provokes, is the becoming-equivocal of memory and perception. It is the becoming-equivocal or becoming-fabulous of the real. The rapport is autonomous because it has no subject or object. It is absolute. It is not a rapport *with* any *thing* (other than its own obsessive "self"). Hence it is the most uncertain of rapports and the most persistent, since it cannot be absorbed into anything determinate or accomplished. It cannot be put behind us because it is a rapport with the nonthing that shimmers "beside" the thing in a space empty of space. It cannot be possessed and put to work in the service of any task, but it can be affirmed—must be affirmed—obliquely, for it is without any self or identity. Every artwork is an oblique affirmation of this rapport that resists definition.

What if this neutralizing space, as close as possible to madness (if not its very possibility and beginning)—this space that discourse itself opens up and maintains and that literature purely and simply affirms—what if this space emptied of all identities were already a community? It would be a strange community, but a community nevertheless. What if that which remains invisible and unperceived was in fact that which *in* any community escapes it such that one always already "belongs" to any community whatever without, however, belonging based on any representable condition? What would it mean to belong to a community purely anonymously? To belong to a community before it is a community *of . . .* (this or that, men, God's creatures, etc.)? A community without any essence or any preconditions of belonging? Giorgio Agamben profiles for us such a community in his remarkable book *La comunità che viene.* He describes a community to which one is called by virtue of pure "being called [l'esser-detto]": the "property [proprietà]," he says "that establishes all possible belonging [che fonda tutte le possibili appartenenze]." This "property" he tells us, is "purely linguistic being [l'essere puramente linguistico]."

Whatever!

The "space" or structure of Agamben's book is crazy, slightly drunk (even as the thinking in it is precise and delicate). Each of its brief three or four page sections, fragments, or panels (like in comic books) attempts to think the same thought under various names: *"Quodlibet ens,"* "Example," "Ease," "Manner," "Halo," *"Shekinah,"* "Bartleby," *"Principium Individuationis,"* "Image," Heidegger's *as*, the *thus*, and the *rather*, among still others. It is important to read each section or panel as superimposed on the others or as if each simultaneously occupied the same space (or perpetually empty *thought*) such that each is a new, disparate perspective but *of* no landscape or argument. We may describe the book as erudite, or as a philosophical serendipity, but that seems beside the point, for it is as if these panels came from elsewhere than one mind or one thinker. The work, if anything, is *variously* erudite, as if Agamben himself (and we know nothing about him personally) were a crazy auto-dictat whose polyvocal erudition always threatened to transform him into a multiple-personality case. But we insist that the sense of almost comical erudition is quite to the point. He is not obsessed so much with an ideé fixe but with an Idea that perpetually *unfixes* thought, so that thoughts themselves become pure perspectives, or images of thought, without forming any one figure.

We may wish to compare *La comunità che viene* to a Balthus street scene where each of the characters in the street quietly occupies its own space and goes about its business but where each seems to be looking into or moving into *different* spaces so that, as we look at the canvas, our gaze is petrified. Our gaze looks into no one space, but rather is transferred from various space to various space, each tangential to the other, but not organically related. In this way, each character becomes simple, serene, absolute, and is possessed by a strange detachment. Our gaze is not merely passive and contemplative. It cannot but get involved since it cannot even find what would be called the space of the canvas. Our eye is drawn *into* the canvas, whose "space" is missing, and which itself, then, becomes an enormous eye staring at us with a gaze emptied of sight. This is Balthus's technique and it was first noticed, as far as we can tell, by Antonin Artaud, who contrasts it to trompe l'oeil.[12] Instead of duping us into believing that something real is there that is not there, Balthus overcomes or overwhelms the distanced passivity of contemplation by *petrifying* the real. He accomplishes this by breaking up perspective into fragments (of no wholes) thus giving his characters the sphinx-like quality that Artaud noticed in his review. One can observe the same thing among children who are each fascinated by, and totally involved in playing with, the same objects but each in his or her own completely singular way. To the adult who watches, this tends to petrify the object and make of it an image of itself. Anyone who has had to tend more than two children at once is aware of the breakup of perception into radical perspectivism and radically pluralized significations. Our perspective is a perspective on that which has returned to its originary image and is without figure, as if our perception were temporarily blinded. We are no longer able to see an image *of* this or that, and our perception is overwhelmed and pulverized by pure perspectivism.

Agamben's fragments, or panels, are all commentaries, he tells us, on an old metaphysical problem: the relation between essence and existence, *quid est* and *quod est*.[13] Each fragment rethinks this problem (which is the problem of intelligibility itself) anew, offers another perspective on the problem, and in each case seeks to liquefy the notion of essence as stable and stabilizing, proper, erect, and unifying. Instead of an *esse*, he attempts to think a "most common" or *the* most common. He attempts to think the Whatever or *Quodlibet* (*qualunque* or *quelconque*), which, his translator cautions us, refers not to the general or the particular, the generic or the individual, but to the "singular" in the sense in which Deleuze and Badiou use the term.[14] The commonality Agamben repeatedly approaches in his fragments both involves us in a "belonging" and also deprives us of any representable condition of belonging. For the Whatever is just that—whatever!

There is nothing mysterious, magical, or ineffable about the Whatever. It is as common as can be. It is the most common. It is not representable or themetizable, not because it is withdrawn, silent, negative, or removed, but *because it is too common*. It is not even hidden, and it offers nothing to be thought, contemplated, or worried about. Thought need not seek after it, for it is already in every thought and in every representation. It is not a generic "given" that we can always fall back on, nor a banal background for any possible community such as "We're all human," or "It's a small world," or "To each his own as long as it doesn't hurt anyone else." The most common, like the *il y a* in Levinas and Blanchot, is what needs to be repeatedly approached and exposed, for the most common *is* only in its approach, its exposure, its "coming." To approach the Whatever is to approach an ever-elsewhere that is not absent, an ever-here that is not present. *Qualunque* is the neutralization of identity that is in every representation while remaining noncontemporary with that representation. It is only glimpsed in profile, or in the shadows of a perception or a feeling.

Whatever being is not a subject, *hypokeimenon*, or substance that underlies all its predicates and is whatever remains when all its qualities are removed. It is not a limit that grounds intelligibility. Whatever being is being such that all its predicates unlimit it infinitely, unground or liberate it infinitely. Whatever being is being that finds itself in its unlimiting. "All its predicates" *un*determine whatever being, unravel it, and expose it such that whatever being can only transcend toward itself infinitely, toward itself such as it is—an empty totality that "all its predicates" (de)constitute and (de)limit. Whatever being is being whose Being is perpetually delayed, retarded, or approached, for "all its predicates" is not a possibility for whatever being. Rather, it is an impossibility that continually shimmers beside it, in an empty imaginary space "reserved" for it but never occupied.

This does not mean that whatever being strives majestically toward all that it can be, toward a utopian self that shimmers in an inaccessible horizon lighting up a path towards an ideal identity. Instead, something quite different happens. Since "all its predicates" is *not* a predicate of whatever being, any particular one of those predicates (being-masculine, being-American, e.g.) exposes a relation between a real being and an *empty* totality, a nonthing, or nothing that renders this real being a *whateverness*. This does not drain whatever being bloodless and make it, like Sartre's *ego*, pure and simple transcendence.[15] It means that whatever being is a pure and empty *relation to language*, to predication, such that only in language *is* whatever being *as* it is, yet without being defined once and for all: not *being* its predicates but *being-called* (this or that, "American," "masculine," e.g.). Whatever being is not its qualities. It is its exposure to *all* its qualities that each particular quality *re*says or *re*-calls. The existence of whatever being is purely linguistic, purely being-called. Thus it is *in* language that whatever being finds itself, suffers itself, touches itself in the pure passion of being-called. It is itself as an empty totality that envelops its real existence as this or that.

This empty totality is not a pure and simple void. It is a nothing or an empty space that is added to, or supplements, any being whatsoever. It is a never present supplement without which no being could be what it is. Any particular being is also "whatever is called . . ." Any particular being of course belongs to some genus of some species such that it can be identified as what it in fact is and can be experienced as such. But—and this is Agamben's insight—it "belongs" to the genus as an *example* of it, as an image or schema-image of any such member of that genus. It is *this* particular *and* it is an *example of* whatever is called this or that particular. It is this particular (house, e.g.) *and* it serves for, or stands in the place of, *whatever is-called* ("house," e.g.). As such it exposes its singularity, its whateverness. It occupies its own, and simultaneously the empty, place of the example. It is a particular and it is *so-called*. It is itself *(idem)* and it is whatever being. This is its second life, its second nature, Agamben says. Insofar as

it is-called, it is neither shown nor meant, is neither this particular nor an insipid generality. It only fills the empty space
of the "whatever is called . . ." As called, as named, as an
example, it is not thematized at all. Necessarily, the example
(or the schema-image) is that *in* language for which there is no
name. It is the *pure* being-in-language of the nonlinguistic, the
unnamable (that is, the nonuniversal that is not a particular,
either). The schema-image is the image of no (representable)
figure. We will learn from our analysis of Kant later in this
chapter that an object is itself *only insofar as it need not appear as in fact it actually does appear*. As such, as an example,
it is "given" all its possibilities as an empty totality (a nonfigure)
that changes nothing but the *sense* of the actual. As an example, a thing is "the event of an outside *[l'evento di un fuori]*,*"
Agamben says, by which it has access to itself *(ipse)*, to "its
face, its *eidos* [il suo volto, il suo *eidos*]" (italics in original).[16]

As exemplary, a being is not defined by qualities except
first by passing through being-called, by passing through the
space of neither the particular nor the universal. Although a
such-and-such will be a particular case, it is understood that it
must serve for all others of the same type, and thus it occupies
the empty place of whatever being—a space that is purely linguistic and in which it communicates with other singularities
unbound by any identity. It is strictly being-called, an
unnamable within any denomination that it may be given. That
is: *it is a pure anteriority or infinite shortage of presence that
radically calls its identity into question*. It is hence cut off from
any real community and yet it is the most-common. It is "*whatever is-called . . .*"

Whatever being is not a *je ne sais quoi*, an obscure quality
no one can put their finger on. It is the thing *with* all its predicates that undefine or delimit it. *Quodlibet ens* is the thing
ipse, but only insofar as it "transcends toward itself" in the

empty space of the example. This empty totality unravels it of identity and singularizes it or "unmakes it according to its image," as Blanchot would say.[17] It is the thing with *all* its relations, *all* its qualities. In the space of the example, the thing *is* "all its relations" and "all its qualities." To borrow from one of Agamben's own examples,[18] this letter *p* that I make here is itself not because it belongs to an ideal *p*-form but because it belongs among, or borders on, *all* the various differences and idiosyncrasies in innumerable versions of *p*. The *p* has identity insofar as it belongs to an alphabetic genus, of course, but it is recognizable as what it is only as engendered by a thousand idiosyncrasies that habitually render it legible. In this way common and proper become indistinguishable from each other. The thousand idiosyncrasies describe an empty interworld within which what is called *p* moves freely and according to its own manner. The empty totality of "its" idiosyncrasies are not its properties but its *im*proprieties—its habitual *resistance* to propriety, which in fact *constitutes* its recognizable appearance on the page. This is its second nature, its singularity. Thus Agamben shows us something that is not established once and for all, eternally, but that which is always *l'entretemps*, delayed or coming amongst "an infinite series of modal variations [una serie infinita di oscillazioni modali]."[19] Each individual *p* opens onto an exemplarity, a singularity, that is its oscillations—a vicarious space where each individual *p* substitutes itself for each other possible *p* such that this particular *p* is incarnated *as* substituted.

In this and in many other ways, Agamben describes community such that each being occupies a particular place that is radically in question as it opens onto another space where each being is always already substituted for another being who is in an always other place. In that "other" space, "beside itself," as exemplary, it communicates with all other singularities.

This is not an *actualized* community. No information is passed along in any real communication. The community communicates only its belonging to the most-common. In the example, singular being is "expropriated of all identity [espropriate di tutte le identità]"[20] and abandoned to pure and simple belonging. (It is not as myself, but as singular, *as other*, that I am exposed to the other. "I," in short, to return to the language of Blanchot, becomes He, *il*, Neuter. The multiple common space described by Agamben remains, in my opinion, close to Blanchotian aesthetics, in spite of Agamben's reservations.)[21]

In Agamben's politics, the expropriation of identity and the transformation—today so inescapable—of the real into its image provide us with an unprecedented opportunity to appropriate the most-common and to experience the fact that *one speaks*.[22] This would also be the very appropriation of (or by) anonymity that animates all of Blanchot's narrators and it perfectly describes Blanchot's meditations on writing and the space of literature. For, when *one* speaks, no one (not he nor she, not this one nor that one) speaks. One becomes whatever or whomever speaker, one becomes speaking-being as such, and not a more- or less-qualified speaker. Indeed, one is depropriated of all determinate qualities and one enters the entire space of discourse, such that the one who speaks cannot be ascertained or identified, but circulates within discourse itself. As pure speaking-being, I speak without anyone's being able to trace my words back to me and hold me accountable for them, even if I stand smack in front of the other person, because the *experience* of speaking-being does not refer to a self that I would be. As speaking-being, unable to refer to any reality, I would speak without having any basis for speaking, any reason to open my mouth. Moreover, I would speak without having anything to communicate. My speech would carry no information intended to inform another speaker, another identity. When I speak, no identity would speak and I would speak an imaginary, absolute language. I would be speaking from the place of the Other who would remain always elsewhere. As such, I would approach the other *as other*, outside any identity, for I would not be the subject of any discourse. "Older" than any *communiqué* would be this rapport with the Other outside intersubjectivity, and completely linguistic being would "come" to us like a long suppressed reminiscence or like a long-suppressed passion. Communication would then be united with this passionate rapport, or for-the-other-ness, in a speech that says nothing, reveals nothing, and that is as a foreign language within one's native tongue (as the narrator of *L'arrêt de mort* experiences).[23] This radical communicativity would "possess" us and open a space that is not-yet colonized by the State.

Community

The fate and destiny of a community (human being) that does not have its origin in itself and cannot find its origin outside itself except in silence, tragedy, or alienation—in short, a *negative* ground—is the subject of Agamben's meditation in his earlier book *Language and Death: The Place of Negativity [Il linguaggio e la morte: Un seminario sul luogo della negatività]*.[24] In that book, he attempts to approach an experience of language that does not rest on a negative foundation and he does not find that experience in either philosophy or poetry. Each of those traditions also traces the human voice through language, but each finds only ineffability, silence, mystery, sacred action, or the tragic division of existence and essence, and the absolute fear of the Hegelian threat of the Negative that magically transforms Nothingness into Being. That is to say, neither philosophy nor poetry is able to grasp the taking-place of language which would be the taking-place of the human (insofar as human being is speaking-being) such that human being would then be *capable* of language, seize the faculty for language, and unite it with his finitude as a completed foundation. But, Agamben says, human being, in fact, *does not have a voice*—a nature, an essence—not even a basically removed, silent, or negative voice (or Voice, as Agamben christens it). In short, there is no original *vouloir dire*, and this, alas, has destined human being to a history and a State (which we now inherit in the form of Capital). Thus, with Nietzsche, Agamben concludes that the Voice must die.[25]

But what is language without a Voice, without a *Sigetics*?[26] What is a language that does not say perfectly and preserve in itself an Unsayable, an Ineffable, a Mystery? What, in short, is a language that does not condemn human being to a State, a *Sacer*, a destiny? What is a language that so impoverishes human being that the "extremely nullifying unveiling [estremo svelamento nullificante]"[27] that we today experience would actually offer us a hope? A hope not for an extreme Having-been that, in the Hegelian Absolute or the Heideggerian *Ereignis*, could be seized and appropriated, but a hope for a Never-having-been, an extreme youth or an absolute infancy such that human being would not yet have been born![28] Such a being—who never has been—would speak a language that does not presuppose work, meaning, or articulation. Such a being, never having been, would be *imaginary*, in that "other" version Blanchot defines for us, and such a language would be ambiguous, since it would and would not be the voice of human being. It would no longer refer back to a *self* human being would be.

Agamben's *La comunità che viene* is an attempt to think beyond the "magical" power of the negative. It attempts to think an experience of language *itself*, transparent to itself,

such that the Voice—the division of nature and culture, deno-
tation and signification, showing and telling, e.g.—is abolished
without a trace. *La comunità che viene* is an attempt to think
habit, our "second nature," in such a way that it is not seized,
but tends toward itself, toward transparency. Agamben's book
is an attempt to think language as *ipse* and not *idem:* language
outside identity, or language as that which has no identity, no
essence. In doing this, Agamben is attempting to think that, if
it is the essence of human being to exist—Heidegger's most
difficult thought—then it is *in* language, which has no essence,
that human being becomes capable of this. Such a language is
merely the *"trite* words that we *have* [le *trite* parole che *abbia-
mo*].”[29] All of his book is an attempt to get "between" existence
and essence into a paraonomastic interworld that transcends
only toward itself and does not refer back to an anterior reality that would remain ineffable and unsayable, nor toward a
fictitious signification that would annihilate the real and un-
veil it as essentially Nothing. This interworld is populated with
beings whose being *is* only *in-language.*

Thought, he tells us, traditionally wants to think either
the existence or the essence. Agamben wants to think their
mutual implication, the erosion of their difference, in the anamorphic "space" between "the named thing and its being-
named, between the name and its reference to the thing: between, that is, the name 'rose' insofar as it signifies the rose
and the rose insofar as it is signified by the name 'rose'.”[30]
This delicate interval is the pure exposure of *this* to *that (quod*
to *quid),* existence to essence, such that their mutual implication is the pure *thusness* of the being, the *ipseity* of the *ens.* He
finds in our era an unprecedented opportunity to seize the
thus: the pure being-in-language of the nonlinguistic. Not pure
being *(ousias tes ousias, substantia sine qualitate)* but pure
being-in-language. The pure relation that is neither denoted

nor meant, neither shown nor said. Neither the subject—the pure relationless being that can only be shown and not said—nor that which is said of the thing in the proposition, but the perfectly *exposed* being that is always already in language, always already hollowed out by representation. This "between" is not the thing in its nonrelational denotatedness, nor the thing in its identity (its meaning). It is the thing itself *(ipse)*. Not pure being, but being-such: the being-such, Agamben says, of the "as" in the question, "what is being as being?" Not, therefore, prelinguistic substance, nor any said, but that which "exists" only as always already hollowed out by representation. Such beings populate Agamben's "coming community."

It may be helpful here to think of that wonderful population whose existence is purely plastic: the Hollywood character actor. These are actors whose names may be known to us (Thelma Ritter, Elisha Cook Jr., Walter Brennan) but much more often than not they remain unknown and forgotten, buried in the credits at the end of the film as we walk out of the theater or push the rewind button. Yet they are ever so familiar and ever so versatile, appearing year after year in movies and on TV shows, in Westerns, Noirs, historical dramas, bio-pics, war pictures, bedroom farces and action potboilers. Character actors are absolutely familiar to us but they never possess "star quality." They never get billing above the title or even on the marquee at all, and they never star in their own television series or even costar. They are not Lon Chaney, who worked so tirelessly at the art of self-disguise that he became a Hollywood legend and even had a film made about him starring James Cagney. Instead, these character actors we have in mind never work hard to disguise themselves or to dissolve into a role as in "method" acting. To the contrary, they play their various roles in much the same way, film after film, year after year, decade after decade. They are actors who become so familiar because their reality is entirely made up of their various roles such that their mannerisms, habits, looks, vocal tonalities, and gestures all become *characteristic* and as familiar as the actors themselves remain unfamiliar to us. These are actors, in short, who *show* us their anonymity and we, in turn, quite appropriately become absolutely indifferent to them. They always play "types" and they are nothing apart from the types they play. They remain so unknown to us not because they hide an essence, but because they are completely exposed. (If you ever trouble yourself to search through the credits for such an actor's name it is probably only because you suddenly realize you've been seeing him or her for years *without realizing it*, and this has nothing to do with their having given a particularly stunning performance.) There is nothing ineffable about these actors. There is no residue of greatness, genius, or even talent that clings to their appearance on the screen. They are a void in the midst of the whole ensemble of actors brought together for the picture. We become accustomed to seeing them, yet we know nothing about them via biographies, cults, tabloids, talk shows, or awards ceremonies. We know them only as images and we see them only as images, that is, as allegories of themselves. Each role is another allegory.

These marvelous actors are therefore singularities. They cannot be distinguished as stars nor identified with a particular role (for each role they play is an echo of all the others—all more or less the same) and they seem perfectly at ease with "themselves." We can appreciate the star or glamour quality of Grace Kelly's presence on the screen and the greatness (if not the genius) of Laurence Olivier's talent—some extraordinary or extracinematic "essence"—but character actors are completely absorbed into the celluloid, the *stock*, the stereotypes they play so perfectly. They are "types" and they have assumed themselves as such. The character actor cannot be identified with any particular role but neither do they evoke nor express anything other than the role. They have a pure relation to cinema.

The experience of the character actor, then, is the experience of pure being-in-language—an experience, Blanchot could say, of the event as an image, that is to say, as nothing other than its qualities but such that these qualities cling to no reality, no identity, and refer only to themselves. Levinas reminds us that reality is already its own such event. We habitually see a thing *as* its image, not through it. Reality, he has told us, is dual—it is itself in its truth *(idem)* and in its image, "like a torn sack that spills its contents."[31] Very similarly, Agamben writes:

It is as if the form, the knowability, the features of every entity were detached from it, not as another thing, but as an *intentio*, an angel, an image. The mode of being of this *intentio* is neither simple existence nor transcendence; it is a paraexistence or a paratranscendence that dwells beside the thing (in all the senses of the prefix 'para-'), so close that it *almost* merges with it, giving it a halo. It is not the identity of the thing and yet it is nothing other than the thing (it is *none-other*).

[È come se la forma, la conoscibilità, la fattezza di ogni ente si staccasse da esso, non come un'altra cosa, ma come un'*intentio*, un angelo, un'immagine. Il modo di essere di questa *intentio* non è una semplice esistenza né una trascendenza: è una paraesistenza o una paratrascendenza, che dimora a fianco alla cosa (in tutti i sensi della preposizione *pará)*, cosí a fianco da

confondersi *quasi* con essa, da nimbarla. Essa non è
l'identità della cosa e, tuttavia, non è altro (è *non altro*)
che questa.][32]

This image, event, singularity, allegory of itself, or Idea
(as Agamben understands it)[33] is being such-as-it-is, its none-
otherness, or its not-otherwiseness. As a character-actor, the
actor becomes his or her own image. Character actors are capable of their not-otherwiseness such that, without any residue,
they neither betray an essence nor a substance they "really"
are, nor do they identify themselves with any one role, but
rather move freely, happily, imperceptibly and irreparably
within the paraonomastic interzone of thusness. They are nothing other than their types, mannerisms, and gestures, and yet
they *are not* these qualities. They have assumed their manner
of being *im*properly, habitually, without assuming this or that
quality as definitive of their identity. They are nicely insouci-
ant, or cynical, or hypocritical with regard to image and reality. They do not struggle to hold the two realms apart, but
rather allow the two realms to implicate each other. They are
themselves the erosion of the distance that would properly
distinguish the real from the image. They are not possessed by
"another me" but instead are neutral with regard to identity
because assuming one's not-otherwiseness means assuming that
which does not refer back to a self, an "I," that one would
truly be. Character actors are at ease with their manner of
being. In this way, the character actor remains rigorously uni-
dentifiable (and not simply buried in the credits at the end of
the film, since to whom would this or that proper name refer,
anyway)? Unlike star presence, character acting "shows" a
nonparticular presence: a dead presence that seems to belong
to no particular film it happens to turn up in.

In the space of the "type," the habitual, or, as Blanchot

could say, the "everyday," the definitive is engulfed and lost and, even more disastrous, the unity of space is shattered, since these "types" communicate with each other without forming an organic community or a unicity. They "form" a motley. That is, these characters do not come together within a unicity, but rather exist side by side as fragments. The space of character actors dissolves the unity of space, and the glamorous presence of the Great Star (Humphrey Bogart in *Casablanca*, Joseph Cotton in *The Third Man*) is always in danger of being drowned by these multiple and singular indifferences to stardom and even to "acting." As in a Balthus street scene, each character actor occupies his or her own scintillating and unique space that threatens to dissolve the narrative into an infinite series of indeterminate and chaotic possibilities. In their ways, character actors communicate destruction: the radical destructiveness of a noncollective, nonidentifiable community. They are each the possibility of still *appearing* when there is no longer anyone to be, no immanence and no identity to belong to.

Character-actors are employed by Hollywood to represent the business and hum of everyday life. They are paid to represent what happens when nothing happens: everydayness. Waiters and waitresses, cabdrivers, cooks, petty crooks, ordinary GIs, musicians, servants, shopkeepers, secretaries, bureaucrats, and stool pigeons: these roles comprise a "petty bourgeoisie" in the Hollywood social economy. Neither extras nor costars, the character actor is forever "between" these two poles. They are not part of a mob, a theater audience, a street crowd; nor are they strewn, bloody and motionless, on any of countless make-believe battlefields. Neither are they ever leads, nor heroes. Belonging to neither class they are, in effect, withdrawn from all classes and they are the possibility of dissolution that threatens both the individual power of the hero or the leader *and also* the power of the collective (who either gravitate toward the hero, or who, acting as one, themselves constitute a power). Character acting is the powerless possibility of dissolution, of neither/nor, of anonymity, that threatens all members of all classes. (On *The Tonight Show with Johnny Carson,* Gene Hackman once anxiously complained that he was becoming a character actor. Johnny quickly reassured him that that couldn't be true, because he had recently won an Academy Award for Best Actor.)

In minor roles and as bit players, character actors always appear as reproduced. When they turn up on the screen our gaze at them is purely superficial, unburdened of the drama of identification that the glamour of the star evokes. *Character actors do not challenge us to see.* They offer our gaze that which remains to be seen when there is nothing to see and our gaze is always satisfied by them, by their indefiniteness, by their soft uncertain presence. These actors manage to be identified neither with their real names nor with any name they may be given in a film. They are the unstable shifters in cinematic grammar. Always "he" or "she," always "the one who we just saw in . . . ," always their next *and* previous roles, they are pure echoes of identity, manifestations of insignificance. When we see them again on the screen, in yet another film or TV show (for they are always and only seen *repeatedly*, never for a first time) they are seen precisely as someone I recognize but had forgotten even existed. But from where do I recognize them? It is difficult to say because they are not identified with any one picture or TV show. (No one goes to the cinema to see an Akim Tamiroff or a Queenie Smith film.) Thus they happen to appear, here and there, now and then, as events of re-cognition, repetition, and difference. Radically depropriated of identity (right in front of our eyes!), radically "imaged," radically stereotyped, they are just as radically "capable" of their depropriation. They are "capable" of impropriety, insignificance, insubstantiality. They do not appropriate their qualities as radically identificatory of themselves. Instead, they are, in-themselves, the pure "taking-place" of those qualities: an ac-tor = *x*, sort of. That is the secret of their lightness and their always familiar but insubstantial "life." While Jackie Gleason's obesity identified him and marked both his comic and dra-matic roles with an uncomfortable pathos, in Sydney Green-street obesity is borne superficially and stereotypically, like a simple play of light and shadow.

Object = x

If *The Coming Community* is, as Agamben says, a commentary on section 9 of *Being and Time* and on proposi-tion 6.44 of Wittgenstein's *Tractatus Logico-Philosophicus*,[34] it is also, in our opinion, thoroughly precedented by Heidegger's *Kant and the Problem of Metaphysics* and in particular the analysis of what he considers to be the "kernel" of the *Cri-tique of Pure Reason*, the Transcendental Schema.[35] In this analysis, Heidegger shows that at the heart of objectivity there is a nonthing, a nonbeing, a nonempirical and unintended "me-dium," or, as Kant calls it, an Object = *x* where the "power" of the transcendental imagination *(Einbildungskraft)* becomes equivocal: equally active and passive, or perhaps purely pas-sionate.[36] The Object = *x*, we shall see, is the essentially objec-tive or exterior character of what is most intimate or interior. It is an always anterior presentation that transforms interior-ity into, as Blanchot would say, "an exterior force that we submit to passively."[37] We shall see that every empirical intu-ition (every "appearance") is haunted by an aspectral presen-tation, or *pure* image, that realizes the possibility of the absence of the object, but that remains nevertheless a rapport with the same object. This other relation is nonpersonal or even, better stated, the icy *exclusion* from the personal. In the work of art, as in the corpse (where what appears *insists* upon the absence and inaccessibility of that which is represented), this "other" relation makes itself obscurely felt. Importantly, this "other" relation is a relation to the *same* thing, a relation with that shadow "behind" appearances that is nothing other than the thing itself. In short, we shall show that one always has a relation with a not-otherwiseness, or irreparability, antecedent to all determinate relations. But that "other" rapport is a rapport with no object. It is a rapport with nothing other than the self itself—but outside of, and exterior to, itself.

According to William Richardson (from whose admirably clear summary of the *Kantbuch* we will borrow heavily in what follows) the key to Heidegger's study of the *First Critique* is his repeated insistence on the finitude of human knowing.[38] The human knower does not create the being-to-be-known. That which is known is always objective in character, is outside the knower, and is not the knower. As finite, human knowing must begin in intuition, sensation, reception, affect, passivity. The "passive" side of knowing is ontologically anterior and primary. But for Kant, as is well known, receptivity is not sufficient for knowledge. The immediate presentation of a singular must be determined to be such or such. As determined, the immediately intuited is then re-presented as what it is in general, in light of universality. This side of knowing is thought. It is active and "spontaneous." From the raw data of intuition the contents of universality are constructed and re-presented. Thought, in general, as Richardson puts it, is a presentation (in concepts) of a presentation (an intuition), and it is even more finite than intuition, since it is ontologically dependent on "raw data." On the other hand, thought is "more" presentative than intuition since it provides a unity that holds good for more than one particular. Human knowing is the intimacy

of these profoundly diverse slopes: passive and multiple intuition, and active and unifying thought. Kant's task is to make
clear how they can possibly be synthesized. We notice straightaway that, although diverse, the two sides have something in
common: each presents, and we know that in Kant the power
of presentation in general belongs to the transcendental imagination as it functions in the mystery of schematizing.

But what can be known? Kant's answer is famous. We
know only the being-that-appears, an ob-ject ob-posed *(Gegen-
stand)* to a knower. We know appearances and, crucially, an
appearance "can be nothing by itself, outside our mode of
representation."[39] However, knowing is not ontically creative.
We do not create that which we know. There is an essential
distance between the knower and the known because the finite
knower does not create the being-to-be-known. A human
knower is not God. Distinct from finite knowing, an infinite
knower does not know objects *at all*. God knows the *Ent-
stand*, the e-ject (i.e., the thing insofar as it takes its origin in
God).[40] God does not know things-that-appear (i.e., objects)
but things as they are, as such, in-themselves *(an sich)*. Infinite
knowing is therefore not so much better than human knowing (than perspectivism) as it is profoundly different, because
no objects are even given to God to be known. To put it differently, unlike the finite knower, God does not have to antici-
pate a being-to-be-known, since God is its origin. Finite knowing, in contrast, is essentially temporal, anticipatory, ahead-
of-itself. The *Ent-stand* is profoundly inaccessible to finite
knowing. If the *Ent-stand* is "behind" appearances this does
not mean that it dimly, continually, obliquely, and distortedly
faces the inferior human knower. *It is not knowable at all.*
(For the ontology of *Sein und Zeit*, Heidegger says it is concealed *[verdeckt]*.) The *Ent-stand* is simply not an object and
hence is not available to be known. Importantly, however, the

Ent-stand is the same thing as the thing that appears. It is the same thing as the object: "[T]he thing-in-itself is not another object but another aspect *(respectus)* of representation with regard *to the same object.*"⁴¹ The *Ent-stand* is the same *essent* as the object. Insofar as the *Ent-stand* stands out from God, it *appears* as ob-posed to the finite knower. Indeed, insofar as the thing appears at all, it insists upon an essential nonknowledge (or "hiddenness" as Heidegger prefers to think of it). For the *Ent-stand* is altogether (and not just partially) inaccessible to human knowing. Our relation to the *Ent-stand* is not a relation of knowledge at all. Finite knowing—beginning from finitude, intuition, receptivity, passivity—does not give us access to things-in-themselves. Nevertheless, that which is known (the object, the thing that appears) is nothing other than the *Ent-stand.* Kant, of course, in the *First Critique,* is concerned less with beings per se than with our way of knowing them as objects. He concerns himself with investigating and defining the a priori structures by which and through which that which stands out from God appears and is accessible to human knowing *as* objective and ob-posed. Such knowing would then simultaneously be a barring of access to the *Ent-stand.* He is not so much concerned with mutual presence and self-presence, or "ontic comportment" (the presence of objects to subjects), as he is interested in that anterior structure that makes the comportment possible, because, as he says, "[i]n the world of sense, however deeply we enquire into its objects, we have to do with nothing but appearances."⁴²

By Kant's account, then, human knowing will constitute *only* that which makes beings into objects and allows us experience them such that that which so constitutes objects will also constitute experience. Our encounter with beings will not create beings nor seize them as God does and know them as they are in-themselves. Anterior (a priori) access is a "fashioning," a "making," an "instituting" of things-*as-objects*. Anterior contact will combine the two sides of knowing, intuition and thought, into a unity. And since, for Kant, this is a "power" of the knower, it will come *from* the knower and thus must simultaneously fashion, make, institute, and experience *itself*. In short, that which *ob*-jectifies also *sub*-jectifies. Neither intuition alone nor thought alone can do this and claim to be the "foundation." Each, taken independently, is always prior to any experience (i.e., is *pure*).

Prior to all experience, the immediate, receptive encounter with a singular results in two types of presentations: space and time. Space and time are intuited but are not objects. They are not explicitly apprehended. Clearly, therefore, that which pure intuition intuits must come from intuition itself. Nonobjects, space and time (outer and inner) are not knowable. Intuiting them, intuition is hence not affected by any object. It is affected by that which it gives to itself. Something is intuited, but not an object. It is not nothing at all, but neither is it anything thematic. Heidegger says simply that in its pure passivity, intuition intuits itself. That is, intuition *is* that which it intuits. It gives itself that which it is able to intuit. Space and time are not "outside" intuition. Intuition is always already *in* that which it receives. Space and time, in short, are pure images.

On the other hand, pure thought, prior to all experience, is the discerning of a unity that more than one individual possesses in common: a concept. But pure concepts (causality, e.g.) have no empirical content (which led Hume, of course, to deny their reality). For Kant, the pure concept (or "notion") is simply a function of unification itself. The "contents" of pure concepts are "rules" (i.e., not empirical intuitions). These rules are not a product of reflection but are the very working of reflection. The rule is an antecedent presentation of unity that guides the concept. As pure, the rules constitute that which they rule. They "disappear" into that which they rule and are nothing outside their work. They inscribe themselves in a something-to-be-ruled (i.e., a something-to-be-unified). The totality of these rules is the categories. A category is a way a rule rules, and the Understanding is simply the closed totality of the ways by which intuitive data can be unified, inscribed, ruled. The *Verstand* is a "power of rules" or a power of ways or manners of presentation. Furthermore, since every act of knowing implies a consciousness, the *pure* concept is the consciousness of a unity and implies a *pure* self-consciousness. Thus, for Kant, all conceptual unities have the character of an "I think." This "I think" is a thinking and not simply an act; it is a "power" (a *potentia*) he calls *transcendental apperception*. That is, transcendental apperception is not an act that comes and goes but a *potentia* that remains in reserve even as it works. It is a stable unity without which there would be no knowledge, for there would be no common point to serve for multiple data. Thus the transcendental apperception is the ground of the possibility of the categories.

Now, since the properly Kantian experience must be *made,* there must be a power that unites pure intuition and pure thought such that a knower *can* experience an object. Since both intuition and thought *present,* Heidegger will look for their root in what they share and, as was said earlier, the faculty of presentation in general is the imagination. *Einbildungs-kraft* is precisely *and only* the ability to "fashion," "image," "institute," "establish," "set up," etc. This *Kraft* is not an established fact but a continual process—*the process of sharing that which pure intuition and pure thought have in common.* The imagination integrates the raw data of pure intuition with the syntheses of conceptualization. This process is an activity called *schematizing,* and it is an activity that is at once sensible

and intellectual; it is a fusing of sensation with intellection. By
means of the transcendental (or imaginary) schema, the thing
is able to appear as an object and be experienced as what it is.
It is Kant's famous

> third thing which is homogenous on the one hand with
> the category, and on the other hand with appearance,
> and which makes the application of the former to the
> latter possible. This mediating representation must be
> pure, that is, void of all empirical content, and yet at
> the same time while it must in one respect be *intellec-
> tual*, it must in another be *sensible*. Such a representa-
> tion is the *transcendental schema*.[43]

With regard to empirical concepts, the schema "produces"
or "prescribes" a nonthematic view, or, as Heidegger calls it, a
schema-image,[44] such that any particular can appear as what
it is without being confined to any of the actual particularities
of its appearance. Agamben, quite appropriately, calls this an
"example."[45] We can hardly do better than William Richardson's explanation of how the schema-image works:

> Across the street is a house. I know it to be a house,
> for it is presented to me by an act of knowledge. By
> reason of this presentation, the house offers me a view
> of itself as an individual existing object encountered
> in my experience, but more than that, it offers a view
> of what a house (any house) looks like. This does not
> mean, of course, that the house has no individuality,
> but only that, in addition to its own individuality the
> house as presented offers a view of what a house *can*
> look like, sc. the "how" of any house at all. It opens
> up for me a sphere *[Umkreis]* of possible houses. To

be sure, one of these possibilities has been actualized by the house that I see, but it need not have been so.[46]

With Richardson, we must emphasize the "can" here, for it indicates a *potentia* and an activity by which a thing *is able* to appear as what it is (i.e., to "reveal itself," in Heideggerian language). Importantly for Richardson, Kant, Heidegger, and Agamben, this pre-scription or "rule-for-a-house" is not a determinate catalog of characteristics proper to a house. It is, in Richardson's words, a "full sketch *[Auszeichen] of the totality* of what is meant by such a thing as 'house'" (emphasis mine).[47] This "view" by which a thing *can* appear as what it is called is, in Agamben's analysis, "purely linguistic": *"[T]he name, insofar as it names a thing, is nothing but the thing, insofar as it is named by the name [il nome, in quanto nomina una cosa, è non altro che la cosa in quanto è nominata dal nome]."*[48] Furthermore, Richardson adds, "the view of which we are speaking here is as such neither the immediate (empirical) intuition of an actual singular object (for it connotes a genuine plurality), nor a view of the concept itself in its unity. The view we are speaking of is not thematized at all."[49]

That is to say, in the language of Agamben:

Neither particular nor universal, the example is a singular object that presents itself as such, that *shows* its singularity. . . . Exemplary is what is not defined by any property, except by being called. Not being red, but being-*called*-red; not being Jacob but being-*called*-Jacob defines the example. Hence its ambiguity, just when one has decided to take it really seriously.

[Né particolare né universale, l'esempio é un oggetto singolare che, per cosí dire, si dà a vedere come tale, *monstra* la sua sua singolarità. . . . . Esemplare è ciò che non è definito da alcuna proprietà, tranne l'esser-detto. Non l'esser-rosso, ma l'esser-*detto*-rosso; non l'esser-Jakob, ma l'esser-*detto*-Jakob definisce l'esempio. Di qui la sua ambiguità, non appena si decida di prenderlo veramente sul serio.][50]

In short, the Kantian schema-image defines the "whatever-is-calledness" that Agamben exploits so ingeniously in his *La comunita che viene*. But we must go further still and return to Heidegger's *Kantbuch*.

By way of the schema, the unity of the empirical concept (the word) is referred to the intuited plurality of possibilities it unifies without, however, being restricted to any one or any set of them. In contrast to this, *pure* intuition—time—is *already unified*. It is instead the pure concepts (the categories) that are many. The schematism of the categories must, therefore, require special kinds of schemata or schemata of a character different from those of empirical intuition. As the pure intuition of time is the presentation of *any* object, the schemata must unite the categories to time so that ontological predicates may be applicable to objects *in general*. That is, the profound unity of time must be vulnerable to various *modes* ("ways") of presentation while remaining *one* time (for, "all times are one time"). Richardson reminds us that this is the most difficult and ambiguous aspect of Heidegger's entire analysis of the *Critique of Pure Reason*. Does he want to say *both* that time is the root of the transcendental imagination and that the transcendental imagination is the root of time? Richardson explains it as follows: since time is already unified, the schemata (the "power" to unify) have nothing to unify. But as time is *already* unified, it is always already schematized, or is the (pure) image of any schema whatsoever. Time is the very scheme of the schema-image and as the schemata are several, each is already temporalized. Thus the schemata "determine time" (or, articulate it) *and* time in-forms that which it is articulated by. Time, as unified, "makes possible" that which articulates it and time *is* only *as* articulated (i.e., fused with categories such that ontological predicates can be applied to any object whatever). That is to say, quite obviously, that thinking in terms of form and content is inadequate to capture this conundrum of activity and passivity. (But in this way we reach another aspect of Agamben's analysis that, in the end, will bring him close to Blanchot's notion of the image, and of *la communauté inavouable* insofar as each predicates his analysis on a *general* weakening of mutual presences.)

Now, if the transcendental schemata make possible the application of ontological categories to "any being whatever," then we must look into the ontological status of this "whatever," for it is *precisely* the ontologically *known*. In short, *what* is an object *in general*?

Kant's answer is simple and disarming. It isn't anything:

> Now we are in a position to determine more adequately our concept of an *object* in general. All our representations have, as representations, their object, and can in turn become objects of other representations. Appearances are the sole objects which can be given to us immediately, and that in them which relates immediately to the object is called intuition. But these appearances are not things-in-themselves; they are only representations, which in turn have their object—an object which cannot itself be intuited by us, and which may, therefore, be named the non-empirical, that is, transcendental object = x.
>
> The pure concept of this transcendental object,

which in reality throughout all our knowledge is always one and the same, is what alone can confer upon all our empirical concepts in general relations to an object, that is, an objective reality." (Latter emphasis mine)[51]

Heidegger will say that the mysterious object = x is a "something of which we know nothing."[52] As an object in general, the x is not any particular object and, like the *Umkreis* "house," it is not determinable. It is the *Umkreis* of any possible object. It is the so-called object, or any object purely insofar as it is called an object. It is what all objects share, but it is in-itself a no-thing, nonbeing, nonobject. It is, in Agamben's language again, "the pure being-in-language of the non-linguistic." It is that which, in any object, objectifies it, envisions it as such, as an object. The object-in-general is purely imaginary, because it is schematized par excellence, yet it is that which is not presented in any presentation. In effect, to borrow from Lyotard: it is the presentation of the unpresentable. Heidegger will call it a "pure horizon" within which any object can be rendered present-to-us. Kant will say it is a "pure correlate" to transcendental apperception insofar as it is a unity waiting for something to unify, a like that precedes anything to liken. In that sense it is *more* objective than any object, more being than any being, so that Heidegger will be able to rechristen it as *Being*. In "Brief über den Humanismus" he says (in my own translation, which I leave crudely literal in order to emphasize the point): "Thus Being is being-er than any being [Gleichwohl ist das Sein seiender als jegliches seiende]."[53] Further, according to Richardson, Heidegger will identify the transcendental imagination as his *Da-sein*.[54]

The object = x is not *a* being, not *an* object, hence its relation to the knower will not be cognitive. It is not present. It is *more* than present; more present than any presentation. It is the sheer "can appear" of any appearance whatever. Not absolutely nothing at all, nor just anything at all, *it is the disjunction of something and nothing.* "This = x," Kant says, "is only the concept of absolute position, not itself a self-subsisting object but only an idea of relation, to posit an object corresponding to the form of intuition."[55] Alien to all substance (i.e., not "self-subsisting"), the object = x is fragility *itself.* Empty of all content, the x is the sheer "that there is" *(il y a, es gibt)* something rather than nothing, just as *Da-sein,* or the transcendental imagination (or, unified apperception), is the sheer "that there is" someone rather than no one. Infinitely fragile, the x is arche-relation, arche-obligation that there be such a thing as imagination (forming, presentation) itself, or any *syn-* itself. Similarly, *Da-sein* is the *being* of the "there," or, the pure position of the self. *Da-sein* is the *being* of the arche-presentation "= x."

This presentation, needless to say, is ambiguous. Nothing, or *the* Nothing, is presented. Nothing is "beyond" it, no thing-in-itself arises ghostlike beyond the objectively known. The x, the sheer presentation, is suspended, delayed, retarded, interrupted—coming but never arriving. The essential distance between the knower and that which is the preeminently ontologically known erodes in such a way that the two sides cannot but fuse together.[56] "Presented" is the return, we can say, with Blanchot and Nietzsche, of what does not come back (into any present). Nothing definitive is presented. No figure, no outline, no border, nothing framed. What "happens" is (only) that the transcendental imagination feels itself obliged to (or constrained to) *present.* That is to say, it feels itself, and thus submits to itself, as if it came from outside itself—*as if it was itself an exterior force.* This auto/heteroaffection is profoundly temporal, moreover, in the sense of an extreme tens(e)-ion, or anticipation. (We must recall from the preceding analysis that, unlike God's knowing, human knowing is temporal.) The "power" of *Einbildungskraft* is here fused with an essential impotence. The object = *x* shares with the *Entstand* the characteristic of unknowability, but, as a presentation *in extremis*, it turns away from God back toward objects, back toward its customary poverty. The object = *x* is the irreparable consignment to things, to objects, to profanity, but only via a detour through the Nothing, through nonbeing. Agamben says, "[T]he human is the one that, being open to the non-thing-like, is, for this very reason, irreparably consigned to things [{l'uomo}, essendo aperto al non-cosale, è, unicamente per questo, consegnato irreparabilmente alle cose]."[57]

We do not then, suddenly and unexpectedly, confront the thing-in-itself, the *sacred* thing, the *Entstand* as it is directly offered from out of the Most Ineffable. To the contrary, we suddenly and unexpectedly confront nothing, nonbeing, that is to say, *ourselves: ourselves as the no-thing "itself."* That which all that *is* has in common is no-thing. We confront a limit without ever confronting it, for the limit was nothing, was always already "in" things, erased in its approach and suspended *en deçà du temps* like a paralyzed and paralyzing force. For that which is presented is the sheer "there," and this pure "there" is the pure position of the Kantian "subject" (which we shall interrogate in the next section of this chapter) or the knower, the transcendental imagination, the *Da-sein.*

Importantly, for Agamben's entire enterprise since *Language and Death*, the (whatever) object = *x* is both the point of subtraction from all language, all identity, all propriety, and also the point of immersion in language-in-general or, simply, the sheer fact that *one speaks*:

Whatever does not therefore mean only (in the words of Alain Badiou) 'subtracted from the authority of language without any possible denomination, indiscernible'; it means more exactly that which, holding itself in simple homonymy, in pure being-called, is precisely and only for this reason unnamable: the being-in-language of the non-linguistic.

[*Qualunque* non significa quindi soltanto (nelle parole di Badiou): 'sottratto all'autorità della lingua, senza nominazione possibile, indiscernible'; esso significa, piú precisamente: ció che, tenendosi in una semplice omonimia, nel puro esser-detto, appunto e soltanto per questo è innominabile: l'esser-nel-linguaggio del non-linguistico.][58]

He makes the immediate addendum to Badiou in order to insure that we do not try to see in this presentation-*in-extremis* a negative presentation, Negative Being, or negative theology. The object = x is the very turning away from the sacred for it is the prepresentation of things, of objects (i.e., of that which is *never* presented to God). If you like, the x "shows" the ungodliness of the world. It shows the irreparable profanity of the world. Via this paralyzed presentation, the world is presented precisely such as it is. Appearances conceal (only the) nothing. No proper nature is revealed to us, no coming-from-out-of-Ineffability is unveiled. In Agamben's language again, only the irreducible "thusness" of things is revealed. Thought, then, before it thinks any thing, is able to think (or is not able not to think) pure profanity, or pure ordinariness, as its *only* extraontic thought.

This means then that (pure) thought is naïveté par excellence. Turning at once to objects, *it has always already forgotten*

God. Irreducibly lost among things, thought—pure being-in-language—is abandoned, undestined, scrupulously thingish. Thought is constrained to think nothing beyond objects. This is its "extreme youth"—to have always already evacuated itself of all latency. Thought is originally purely exposed, purely presented, purely *there*, and it is "able" to hold itself just *en deçà du temps*, or *l'entretemps*, prior to its "work" of figuration. Thought, in short, before it is captured in the world, "thinks" the place of art, *l'espace littéraire*. It is "able" to think, before there is any *thing*, "relation in general" in the pure "there," or *il y a*. This "ability" is a passivity. It is a pure passion. A passion, however, that is never present like a state-of-mind. It is the pure finding-myself-there, or being-the-there. It cannot not be-the-there (without purely and simply ceasing to be). That is to say, for a paralyzed moment, purely exposed to *all* its possibilities (all its predicates) it is undestined to any one or any set of them. But this paralyzed moment does not belong to a past, a "was." *Da-sein*, or the Kantian "subject," *is* its *there* incessantly, without, however, being able to bring itself before itself. It is, as Heidegger says, "ahead of itself."

In a certain sense, we could say that it is the very "work" of whatever being precisely to unwork and undetermine itself by holding itself in "perfect homonymity." At least, Agamben would have us think so, and in his own way he relates whatever beings, "tricksters or fakes, assistants or 'toons [*tricksters* o perdigiorno, aiutanti o *toons*]"[59] (italics and English in original) to the Blanchotian writer, as we have already discussed in our previous chapters. When "expropriated of all identity, so as to appropriate belonging itself [espropriate di tutte le identità, per appropriarsi dell'appartenenza stessa],"[60] whatever being, like the writer, is subtracted from all (representable) commonality, all identifiable community, and becomes radically "capable" of instability, fragility—that is, relation-in-general.

With the expropriation of all "contents," all "latency," this pure relation is obscurely felt. The work of art, as Levinas has shown, realizes such a detachment from conditions. It realizes sheer appearance. Radically unseizable, art realizes the extreme possibility of *another* relation that Agamben historicizes in his *La comunità che viene*. His "coming" community is nothing other than the sheer, immanent possibility of being-in-language insofar as language offers neutrality, anonymity, indifference with regard to identity. It offers the speaker the "ability" to no longer say "I," just as Blanchot has written.[61]

Our era, writes Agamben, is one in which all reality has been transformed into its image. Glamorous and alienating, the spectacle has totalized itself and forever separated human life from the possibility of a presupposed common Good. Our "nature"—the fact that we speak—has been expropriated and commodified and nothing of God, nothing of the sacred, had been revealed in this "extremely nullifying unveiling [estremo svelamento nullificante]."[62] In our era, communication occupies its own "autonomous sphere [sfera autonoma]"[63] (Baudrillard's "hyperreality"). The "word"—the "power" to reveal anything whatsoever—has acquired its own materiality and has become a commodity. Language, the Most Common, has been taken from us and has revealed only the nothingness of all things. Yet a hope and an intervention remain possible for us.

To begin with, lived experience has long since been distanced in advance and hollowed out by representation. (It was Walter Benjamin who noticed those tourists, standing with their cameras in front of great works of art, preserving an experience they would never have.) This means that the Spectacle (representation in general) is the pure form of separation: "[W]hen the real world has been transformed into an image and images become real, the practical power of humans is separated from itself and presented as a world unto itself [dove il mondo reale si è trasformato in un'immagine e le immagini diventanto reali, la potenza pratica dell'uomo si distacca da se stessa e si presenta come un mondo a sé]."[64] This *mondo a sé* has been captured and regulated by a competitive mediacracy that now manipulates and controls the perception and the memory of the community. Humans, henceforth, are separated from their Most Common—language, *Logos.* Furthermore, Agamben argues, this mammoth, magnificent expropriation has emptied the world of all beliefs, traditions, contents, latency, and sacredness and has replaced them with products. It has revealed the nothingness of all things (i.e., it has revealed that what was "hidden" in all things—"behind appearances"—was only the susceptibility of all things to becoming their own image, their own appearance. What was "hidden" was not some essence, but sheer spectrality.)

That which has been expropriated from humans now comes back to them commodified, worked over and revaluated by the media *because language is dead and has become its own image.* Our linguistic "nature" comes back to us inverted: as art, as unnatural, as not-ours. In its "work" of emptying out beliefs and traditions, language *itself* remains nevertheless hidden and separated from us.

For this very reason, Agamben argues, it is now possible for us to experience language itself—not this or that content of language, not this or that true or false proposition, but the sheer fact that "one speaks." Language—that which unveils—remains in our era, still veiled. What remains unseen and unexperienced is that communication, emptied of all content, "is able" to communicate *itself.* The sinking into nullity of the real communicates no message, no destiny, nothing sacred. It communicates only the fragility of being-in-relation. This means that it communicates obsessively, incessantly, and exclusively *the impossibility of exclusion.* This is Agamben's "lesson" for us and his quasi difference from Blanchot. More "positively" than Blanchot, he says that the community of those who have no common, representable commonality is the return of nonexclusion. Its eternal return.

In our era, then, it is no longer the sacred dead who reveal community to us as we gather together in a single (de)composing throng.[65] It is the real itself that now incessantly dies— in its image, its corpse, in language itself. Experience is long since dead. There is (only) (the) nothing left to experience— ourselves, in short. Only those "capable" of such an experience will enter Agamben's community *che viene* unharmed. The political task that remains is destruction. The appearance of the *autonomy* of the mediatized spectacle must be destroyed. Like the sacred, and like the *Sigetic* Voice, the commodity/ spectacle must be ushered to the grave: "[T]o link together image and body in a space where they can no longer be separated, and thus to forge the whatever body, whose *physis* is resemblance—this is the good that humanity must learn to wrest from commodities in their decline [compenetrare immagine e corpo in uno spazio in cui essi non possano essere piú separati e ottenere cosí in esso forgiato quel corpo qualunque, la cui *physis* è la somiglianza, questo è il bene che l'umanità deve saper strappare alla merce al tramonto]."[66]

Politics

Far from lamenting the loss of experience, the weakening of mutual presence and self presence, the expropriation of our linguistic nature, and our consequent alienation (adrift in hyperspace, Baudrillard would say), Agamben asks us to welcome it. We must welcome it because this alienation alone can "restore" us to ourselves, to ourselves insofar as we are *originally* expropriated of language and experience.

Being-expropriated *is* human being. That is to say, at the end
of the era of Capital and its magnificent concentration in the
Spectacle, the being that returns and the community that comes
is the one paradoxically "constituted" or "instituted" *by* expropriation. It is the being whose reality is purely linguistic
and (para)transcendental. This being, this community, has no
being proper to it except for its (para)transcendental bordering on all its possibilities. Such a being is fragile, unstable (an-
archic, as Levinas would say)—*the pure possibility of any relation whatever*. It is a being constituted *by* expropriation and
also, simultaneously, by the impossibility of exclusion because
it incessantly borders on all its possibilities. Without destiny
and without essence, the community that returns is one never
present in the first place. Presubjective in the proper sense,
this community is *qualunque!* Infinitely vulnerable, dependent
on the supplement, we will have been offered, in the end, the
possibility to appropriate our expropriation itself, by "holding ourselves in simple homonymity."

In our analysis of Kant, we have seen that the transcendental apperception cannot grasp an object. The sole "content" of its knowing is always the "same," the object = x: "A
something of which we can know nothing," Heidegger says.
Deprived of any actual object, transcendental apperception
can only "think" a pure "there" or a "pure position" that, in
fact, it itself is. Deprived of even intellectual content (or intellectual intuition—something Kant never admits into his philosophy), this "perfectly contentless representation," he says,

> Cannot even be called a conception, but merely a con-
> sciousness which accompanies all conceptions. By this
> I, or It, who or which thinks, nothing more is repre-
> sented than a transcendental subject of thought = x,
> which is cognized only by means of thoughts that are

predicates, and of which, apart from these, we cannot form the least conception. Hence we are obliged to go round this representation in a perpetual circle, inasmuch as we must always employ it, in order to frame any judgment respecting it. And this inconvenience we find it impossible to rid ourselves of, because consciousness in itself is not so much a representation governing a particular object as a form of representation in general. . . .[67]

Like the object = x, the subject = x is inconceivable outside its predications. It is nothing other than its predications, yet it is not purely and simply its predications. The subject = x is "like" the object = x to the extent of being likeness *itself*, (i.e., always the Same, likeness or resemblance is its *physis*). It is a pure resemblance resembling nothing, no thing, no object. A mere x, this transcendental subject is not knowable or experienceable in itself. The transcendental apperception is a nothing that can grasp nothing. It is that which makes possible experience, but it itself is subtracted from any experience. We must note Kant's reluctance to identify it definitively. It is, exactly, *a* consciousness: I, He, She, or It. Always the Same, it *has* no identity. It is always the Same x, the Same nothing. That which unites intuition and makes experience "mine" is without any identifiable self. At the heart of Kantian *jemeinigkeit*, then, is an ineliminatable strangeness. "Mineness" is an intimacy exterior to myself. This stranger cannot be excluded, for "we must always employ it, in order to frame any judgment respecting it." The pure I is x, *It*: too weak to grasp itself or know itself in its *own* experience of itself. Its unity is purely *thought*, but not objectified, and hence it remains unrecognized. In framing itself it simultaneously eludes its own grasp. It is a parenthesis that includes all but itself. As enframed, it is empty of itself and is thus the pure border or limit between both pure senselessness and supersensority, on the one hand, and chaotic sensation, on the other. In this way, we reencounter the paradox of time that in-forms that which articulates it (the categories, e.g.) such that there is no time that is not always already articulated and also no category that is not always already temporalized.

For Kant, the pure contentless "representation I," the *Umkreis* or the "I think" that accompanies all representations and makes them mine, remains unexaminable and is purely and simply *named* a transcendental "subject"—the pure subject of the verb, in short, a *text*. But by what magic does Kant identify the transcendental imagination as the "I" *of language?*

In an earlier book, *Infancy and History: Essays on the Destruction of Experience [Infanzia e storia: Distruzione dell' esperienza e origine della storia]*, Agamben calls our attention to Hamann's metacritique of Kant's *Critique of Pure Reason.* Hamann asks: how pure *is* Pure Reason? As we learn from Agamben's resuscitation of the argument, for Kant the pure geometric unity of the "there" seems just naturally to belong to language, so that "transcendental and linguistic seem to merge [trascendentale e linguistico sembrano confondersi]."[68] It was Hamann, according to Agamben, who first suggested the necessity of contaminating Kantian purity by examining its hidden (or, Lacan might say, its "forgotten") relation to language. He says it simply and dramatically: "Reason is language, *logos*. This is the marrow bone at which I shall gnaw until I die of it."[69] From Hamann's intuition, Agamben takes us directly to the notion, elaborated by Benveniste, that it is in and through language that the transcendental subject is instituted. With impressive simplicity, Benveniste declares, "He who says ego is ego."[70] Prior to any experience, transcending any empirical experience, is the *saying* of "I." The transcendental subject is not a pure unity unifying itself. It is the enunciator.[71] That which Kant described as subject = x needed to be supplemented and rethought as the one who *says* "I." Kant's subject = x, *to be a subject*, had to speak (itself). But this leaves us with a question: if it is not (yet) a subject (until it enunciates itself), what or whom did Kant catch a transcendental glimpse of?

The pure "there" of transcendental apperception offers no characteristic that would make it *mine*, my "I." The pure being-there is not available to any subject, but to a mere "there must be someone" (and, moreover, someone ex-scribed, someone who *loses* the *power* to say "I"). This pure position certainly does not realize the immediate representation of "myself," but in fact realizes the absence of "myself," as we have already noted. What is more, the sheer possibility in general of any spatiotemporal relation is radically and originarily inaccessible to any subject. The transcendental apperception— I, He, She, or It—is not a supraconcept that includes all "I's" under its umbrella. It is not a concept at all. Nor a supragenus, nor a set of all sets. It is precisely the rigorous impossibility of any such concept, of any supersensory generality. Totally devoid of all content, of all experience, yet not absolutely nothing at all, this transcendental apperception is the Same as Heidegger's *Da-sein* whose "who" is always in question.[72] It cannot experience itself *as* itself and it is the very eclipse of autoaffection. Radically suspended, the *Da-sein*, being-the-there, is just as radically disinherited. Transcendental apperception, the pure "there," (de)constitutes the "I" that institutes itself in language by interrupting it incessantly—by paralyzing and neutralizing it. Kant's transcendental apperception had to be supplemented by language in order to institute an "I," a subject. That which accompanies all my representations and makes them mine has to *say* "I." But to whom, or to what reality, will this "I" refer?

Benveniste answers, rigorously, "To something very singular, which is exclusively linguistic: *I* refers to the act of individual discourse in which it is uttered and it designates its speaker . . . the reality it evokes is the reality of discourse."[73]

The fleeting and pure "I" that Kant attempted to posit in transcendental apperception was never anywhere but in language. The transcendental *subject*, in the end, was to have been made up of words. The *Umkreis* was language. It was therefore language that stole from me all *my* experiences ab ovo. *I* was never anywhere but in my *saying* "I." The subject was spoken, uttered: He who said "I." All experience, in short, was always already speech. *There is no prelinguistic subject, no dumb experience, and no transcendence otherwise than in language.* The subject is purely linguistic being.

What Kant caught a glimpse of, therefore, was not at all transcendent, but not-yet transcendence, not-yet language. What Kant caught a glimpse of was an impotence or an originary *dependence* on language. What Kant sketched out for us was a not-yet subject, a He, She, or It that *has yet* to speak and is therefore *not* purely and simply embedded in language. He caught a glimpse of that which must *enter* language and whose impotence is its impotent "power" to *think* (but not to circumscribe, or limit) its "must speak." That is to say, Kant describes for us, in light of Benveniste, in light of language, or, more simply, in light of Light itself, that which has no Voice, is given no Voice, but must appropriate language nonetheless in order to be itself. That is to say, *it must appropriate that which will expropriate it of all "mineness."* "Older" than subjectivity is that which, in human being, precedes language. Not a "wordless" experience, sacred and mysterious, but the experience of language *itself.*

It is not outside language, but at its limit that Agamben seeks to provoke a politics. The coming being is not another version of the subject, nor a new foundation, nor a pure and simple absence of foundation. Coming being is the being that enters language and whose "transcendence" is its complete absorption, without residue, in language. It is the being whose Being *is* its bordering on language, on "all its predicates." You see, there is in fact an experience that "remains" when all experience has been expropriated. That experience is the experience of expropriation *itself*, or language, for language is the expropriation of all particular experiences and is the sheer possibility of any particular experience. Not this or that content of language, not this or that true or false proposition, but the sheer and fragile fact that "one speaks." The coming being will be "capable" of its absorption, without remainder, in language. It will at the same time "retain" this "capability" (or *potentia*) and think language as such. Both active and passive will fuse into a single passion. Such a being will remain "capable" of its passivity. It will always think, not itself (in its identity that language simultaneously offers and withdraws) but the Same—always the Same experience of expropriation and alienation *as* original.

Because I am *able* to enter language (and there is nothing else for human being to enter), I am also able to think this entry. I am able to think the return of language to language. Such thinking involves, as Blanchot has repeatedly shown, "a loss of the power to say 'I'," and thus an immersion in fascination and a contact with an absolute milieu. No longer to be able to say "I" *is* to think the Same (no one, any one, the Neuter). The region of Agamben's politics is the region of Blanchot's "Essential Solitude"[74]—emptied of subject and object and radically impersonal like Thomas's encounter in the first chapter of *Thomas L'obscur* that Levinas celebrated as so fine a description of the *il y a*.[75] For if the entry into language establishes all possible belonging or relation-in-general (that

which, in short, bears upon any politics or any ethics whatever), it simultaneously depropriates us of any particular relation, politics, or ethics. And thus politics is *exposed*. Any particular politics, or any politics as usual, as we cynically say (as
if it were an autonomous sphere closed to us), is only politics
so-called (as we must learn to say if we are to enter it and
destroy its phantasmic autonomy).

That which is offered us is always the Same: not an essence, a shining path, nor a destiny, but the sheer possibility
of relation *in general*—a dice throw. Any particular politic or
ethic is a point of contact with an absolute milieu empty of all
determinacy. Any particular politics is also the face, the *eidos*,
of "any relation at all." With the notion of radical passivity
we have attempted throughout this book to describe a *general*
rapport or an imaginary dimension where we have never been
but to which we are exposed prior to our subjective intentions. The uncanny "ability" to think this rapport is the "ability" to think that which always comes. Not the masses, nor
the horde, nor the wolves, and not the hero, nor the individual, nor the survivor. The motley.

Notes

Introduction

1. Emmanuel Levinas, "Philosophy and Awakening," trans. Mary Quaintance, in *Who Comes After the Subject?*, ed. Eduardo Cadava, Peter Connor, and Jean-Luc Nancy (New York: Routledge, 1991), p. 215.

2. Emmanuel Levinas, "The Servant and Her Master," trans. Michael Holland, in *The Levinas Reader*, ed. Seán Hand (Cambridge: Basil Blackwell, 1989), p. 159 n. 3.

3. Emmanuel Levinas, "Being and the Other: On Paul Celan," trans. Stephen Melville, *Chicago Review* 29, nos. 16–21 (winter 1978): 16.

4. Maurice Blanchot, "The Outside, the Night," trans. Ann Smock, in *The Space of Literature* (Lincoln: University of Nebraska Press, 1982), pp. 164–67; idem, "La dehors, la nuit," in *L'espace Littéraire,* Idées ser. (Paris: Gallimard, 1955), pp. 220–22.

Chapter One. The Allegory of Being

1. Emmanuel Levinas, "Reality and Its Shadow," trans. Alphonso Lingis, in Hand, ed., *Levinas Reader,* p. 133; idem, "La

réalité et son ombre," *Les Temps Modernes* 4, no. 38 (November 1948): 774.

2. Levinas, "Reality and Its Shadow," p. 133; idem, "La réalité et son ombre," p. 775.

3. Levinas, "Reality and Its Shadow," p. 132; idem, "La réalité et son ombre," p. 774.

4. Levinas, "Reality and Its Shadow," p. 133; idem, "La réalité et son ombre," pp. 774–75.

5. Levinas, "Reality and Its Shadow," pp. 133–34; idem, "La réalité et son ombre," p. 775.

6. Maurice Blanchot, "The Song of the Sirens," trans. Lydia Davis, in *The Gaze of Orpheus*, ed. P. Adams Sitney (Barrytown, N.Y.: Station Hill Press, 1981), pp. 105–13; idem, "Le chant des Sirènes," in *Le livre à venir*, Idées ser. (Paris: Gallimard, 1971), pp. 9–19.

7. Levinas, "Reality and Its Shadow," p. 134; idem, "La réalité et son ombre," p. 777.

8. Levinas, "Reality and Its Shadow," p. 134; idem, "La réalité et son ombre," p. 776.

9. This is hardly the place to summarize Philippe Lacoue-Labarthe's carefully nuanced work on the question of mimesis. We only wish to note that he studies various attempts to restrict, reduce, ignore, or decide on mimesis, and he characterizes each of these attempts as profoundly *political* or *moral* gestures. See especially his "Typography," trans. Eduardo Cadava, "Diderot: Paradox and Mimesis," trans. Jane Popp, and "Transcendence Ends in Politics," trans. Peter Caws, in *Typography: Mimesis, Philosophy, Politics*, ed. Christopher Fynsk (Cambridge: Harvard University Press, 1989); see as well idem, *Heidegger, Art and Politics: The Fiction of the Political*, trans. Chris Turner (Cambridge: Basil Blackwell, 1990).

10. Levinas, "Reality and Its Shadow," pp. 134–35; idem, "La réalité et son ombre," p. 777.

11. Levinas, "Reality and Its Shadow," p. 135; idem, "La réalité et son ombre," p. 778.

12. Levinas, "Reality and Its Shadow," p. 141; idem, "La réalité et son ombre," p. 786.

13. Giorgio Agamben, *The Coming Community*, trans. Michael

Hardt, Theory Out of Bounds ser. (Minneapolis: University of Minnesota Press, 1993), pp. 97–98. *La comunità che viene* (Torino: Giulio Einaudi Editore, 1990), pp. 69–70.

14. Maurice Blanchot, "Two Versions of the Imaginary," trans. Lydia Davis, in Sitney, ed., *Gaze of Orpheus*, pp. 82–85; idem, "The Two Versions of the Imaginary," trans. Ann Smock, in *Space of Literature* , pp. 257–60; idem, "Les deux versions de l'imaginaire," in *L'espace littéraire* , pp. 346–49.

15. Levinas, "Reality and Its Shadow," p.136; idem, "La réalité et son ombre," p. 779.

16. Levinas, "Reality and Its Shadow," p. 141; idem, "La réalité et son ombre," p. 787.

17. Levinas, "Reality and Its Shadow," p. 135; idem, "La réalité et son ombre," p. 778.

18. Levinas, "Reality and Its Shadow," p. 137; idem, "La réalité et son ombre," p. 781.

19. Levinas, "Reality and Its Shadow," p. 137; idem, "La réalité et son ombre," p. 782.

20. Levinas, "Reality and Its Shadow," p. 139; idem, "La réalité et son ombre," p. 783–84.

21. Levinas, "Reality and Its Shadow," p. 138; idem, "La réalité et son ombre," p. 782.

22. Levinas, "Reality and Its Shadow," p. 138; idem, "La réalité et son ombre," p. 782 (emphasis mine).

23. On this point see Jacques Derrida, "At this very moment in this work here I am," trans. Ruben Berezdivin, in *Re-Reading Levinas*, ed. Robert Bernasconi and Simon Critchley (Bloomington: Indiana University Press, 1991), pp. 11–48; see also John Llewelyn, "Levinas, Derrida and Others *Vis-à-vis*," in *The Provocation of Levinas*, ed. Robert Bernasconi and David Wood (New York: Routledge, 1988), pp. 153–54.

24. Blanchot, "Two Versions of the Imaginary," trans. Davis, p. 87; idem, "The Two Versions of the Imaginary," trans. Smock, p. 261; idem, "Les deux versions de l'imaginaire," p. 352.

25. Levinas, "Reality and Its Shadow," p. 139; idem, "La réalité et son ombre," p. 784.

26. Levinas, "Reality and Its Shadow," p. 140; idem, "La réalité et son ombre," p. 785.

27. Levinas, "Reality and Its Shadow," p. 139; idem, "La réalité et son ombre," p. 784.

28. Levinas, "Reality and Its Shadow," p. 140; idem, "La réalité et son ombre," p. 786.

29. Levinas, "Reality and Its Shadow," p. 140; idem, "La réalité et son ombre," p. 785.

30. Levinas, "Reality and Its Shadow," p. 141; idem, "La réalité et son ombre," p. 786.

31. Levinas, "Reality and Its Shadow," p. 141–42; idem, "La réalité et son ombre," p.787.

32. Levinas, "Reality and Its Shadow," p. 142; idem, "La réalité et son ombre," p. 788.

33. Levinas, "Reality and Its Shadow," p. 142; idem, "La réalité et son ombre," p. 788.

34. The notion of an "interruption of myth" that Levinas puts forward here has recently been developed in an essay by Jean-Luc Nancy entitled "Myth Interrupted," trans. Peter Connor, in *The Inoperative Community*, ed. Peter Connor, Theory and History of Literature ser. (Minneapolis: University of Minnesota Press, 1991), pp. 43–70; and also in an essay on Paul Celan by Philippe Lacoue-Labarthe entitled "Catastrophe," trans. Andrea Tarnowski, in *Word Traces: Readings of Paul Celan*, ed. Aris Fioretos (Baltimore: The Johns Hopkins University Press, 1994), pp. 130–56.

35. Levinas, "Reality and Its Shadow," p. 132; idem, "La réalité et son ombre," p. 773: "[A]rt does not belong to the order of revelation. Nor does it belong to that of creation, which moves in just the opposite direction [l'art n'appartient pas à l'ordre de la révélation. Ni, d'ailleurs, à celui de la création dont le mouvement se poursuit dans un sens exactement inverse]."

36. Levinas, "Reality and Its Shadow," p. 142; idem, "La réalité et son ombre," p. 788.

37. Levinas, "Reality and Its Shadow," p. 137; idem, "La réalité et son ombre," p. 781.

38. Blanchot, "Two Versions of the Imaginary," trans. Davis, p.

87; idem, "The Two Versions of the Imaginary," trans. Smock, p. 262; idem, "Les deux versions de l'imaginaire," p. 350 (italics in original).

39. Levinas, "Reality and Its Shadow," p. 141; idem, "La réalité et son ombre," p. 786.

40. Blanchot, "Two Versions of the Imaginary," trans. Davis, p. 87; idem, "The Two Versions of the Imaginary," trans. Smock, p. 262; idem, "Les deux versions de l'imaginaire," p. 352.

41. Michel Foucault, "Maurice Blanchot: The Thought from Outside," trans. Brian Massumi, in *Foucault/Blanchot* (New York: Zone Books, 1987), p. 17.

Chapter Two. Levinas's Ethics

1. Emmanuel Levinas, *Otherwise than Being or Beyond Essence,* trans. Alphonso Lingis (The Hague: Martinus Nijhoff, 1981), p. 191 n. 3; idem, *Autrement qu'être ou au-delà de l'essence* (The Hague: Martinus Nijhoff, 1974), p. 86 n. 3.

2. Levinas, *Otherwise than Being or Beyond Essence,* pp. 50, 136–40; idem, *Autrement qu'être ou au-delà de l'essence,* pp. 64, 174–79 (italics in original).

3. Emmanuel Levinas, "Bad Conscience and the Inexorable," trans. Richard A. Cohen, in *Face to Face with Levinas,* ed. Richard A. Cohen (Albany: State University of New York Press, 1986), pp. 36–40; idem, "La mauvaise conscience et l'inexorable" in *De Dieu qui vient à l'idée* (Paris: Vrin, 1982), pp. 258–65.

4. Emmanuel Levinas, "Dialogue with Emmanuel Levinas," trans. Richard Kearney, in *Face to Face with Levinas,* p. 21.

5. Mikkel Borch-Jacobsen, "Écoute," *Poésie* 35 (1986): 110.

6. Levinas, *Otherwise than Being or Beyond Essence,* p. 11; idem, *Autrement qu'être ou au-delà de l'essence,* p. 14.

7. Martin Heidegger, *Nihilism,* vol. 4 of *Nietzsche,* trans. Frank A Capuzzi, ed. David Farrell Krell (San Francisco: Harper and Row, 1982), pp. 96–118.

8. Levinas, *Otherwise than Being or Beyond Essence,* p. 8; idem, *Autrement qu'être ou au-delà de l'essence,* p. 10.

9. It should be clear even from our analysis so far that the language of Levinas translates nicely into the Heideggerian German of *Sein und Zeit*. This paragraph and the entire discussion of alterity echoes Heidegger's *Ruf (Anruf, Aufruf)* and his *Schuldigsein*. At the end of this chapter, we will take up the question of Levinas's affinity (and aversion) to Heidegger.

10. Levinas, *Otherwise than Being or Beyond Essence*, p. 25; idem, *Autrement qu'être ou au-delà de l'essence*, p. 32.

11. Levinas, *Otherwise than Being or Beyond Essence*, p. 69; idem, *Autrement qu'être ou au-delà de l'essence*, p. 86.

12. Levinas, *Otherwise than Being or Beyond Essence*, p. 148; idem, *Autrement qu'être ou au-delà de l'essence*, p. 189.

13. Heidegger, *Nihilism*, pp. 102–10.

14. Two impressive books by Michel Henry take up this thesis: *The Essence of Manifestation*, trans. Girard Etzkorn (The Hague: Martinus Nijhoff, 1973) and *Généalogie de la psychanalyse* (Paris: Presses Universitaires de France, 1985); but see also Mikkel Borch-Jacobsen's insightful summary and critique of the argument, "The Unconscious Nonetheless," trans. Douglas Brick, in *The Emotional Tie* (Stanford, Calif.: Stanford University Press, 1992), pp. 123–54.

15. Levinas, *Otherwise than Being or Beyond Essence*, p. 124; idem, *Autrement qu'être ou au-delà de l'essence*, p. 159.

16. Levinas, *Otherwise than Being or Beyond Essence*, p. 58; idem, *Autrement qu'être ou au-delà de l'essence*, p. 75 (italics in original).

17. Levinas, "Dialogue with Emmanuel Levinas," p. 28.

18. Mikkel Borch-Jacobsen, "The Freudian Subject: From Politics to Ethics," trans. Richard Miller and X. P. Callahan, in *Emotional Tie*, pp. 15–21; on this point see also Jean Luc-Nancy and Philippe Lacoue-Labarthe, *The Title of the Letter*, trans. François Raffoul and David Pettigrew (Albany: State University of New York Press, 1992).

19. Levinas, *Otherwise than Being or Beyond Essence*, p. 104; idem, *Autrement qu'être ou au-delà de l'essence*, p. 132–33.

20. Levinas, *Otherwise than Being or Beyond Essence*, p. 106; idem, *Autrement qu'être ou au-delà de l'essence*, p. 135.

21. Levinas, *Otherwise than Being or Beyond Essence*, p. 112; idem, *Autrement qu'être ou au-delà de l'essence*, p. 143.

22. Borch-Jacobsen, "The Unconscious Nonetheless," pp. 150, 197 n. 45; see also Mikkel Borch-Jacobsen, *The Freudian Subject*, trans. Catherine Porter (Stanford, Calif.: Stanford University Press, 1988), p. 26ff.

23. Borch-Jacobsen, "The Freudian Subject," p. 26.

24. François Roustang, foreword, trans. Catherine Porter, to Borch-Jacobsen, *Freudian Subject*, p. ix.

25. Levinas, *Otherwise than Being or Beyond Essence*, p. 16; idem, *Autrement qu'être ou au-delà de l'essence*, p. 20.

26. Lacoue-Labarthe, "Diderot: Paradox and Mimesis," p. 259.

27. Levinas, *Otherwise than Being or Beyond Essence*, p. 59; idem, *Autrement qu'être ou au-delà de l'essence*, p. 76.

28. Levinas, *Otherwise than Being or Beyond Essence*, p. 114; idem, *Autrement qu'être ou au-delà de l'essence*, p. 146.

29. Agamben, *Coming Community*, p. 43; idem, *La comunità che viene* , p. 30.

30. Levinas, *Otherwise than Being or Beyond Essence*, p. 193 n. 35: "No language other than ethics could be equal to the paradox which phenomenological description enters when, starting with the disclosure, the appearing of a neighbor, it reads it in its trace, which orders the face according to a diachrony which cannot be synchronized in representation;" idem, *Autrement qu'être ou au-delà de l'essence*, p. 120 n. 35: "Aucun langage autre qu'éthique n'est à même d'égaler le paradoxe où entre la description phénoménologique qui, partant du dévoilement du prochain, de son apparaître, le lit dans sa trace qui l'ordonne visage selon une diachronie non-synchronisable dans le représentation."

31. Georges Bataille, *The Tears of Eros*, trans. Peter Connor (San Francisco: City Lights Books, 1989), p. 206ff.

32. Much of this discussion of Levinas's ethics (and much of my understanding of Blanchot) owes its inspiration to two sensitive articles by William Flesch: "Proximity and Power: Shakespearean and Dramatic Space," *Theater Journal* 39, no. 3 (October 1987); idem, "Posthumous Sadness," unpublished paper.

33. Quoted by Maurice Blanchot in *The Unavowable Community*, trans. Pierre Joris (Barrytown, N.Y.: Station Hill Press, 1988), p. 9; idem, *La communauté inavouable* (Paris: Les Éditions de Minuit, 1983), p. 21 (italics in original).

34. Levinas, *Otherwise than Being or Beyond Essence,* p. 193 n. 33; idem, *Autrement qu'être ou au-delà de l'essence,* p. 116 n. 33. In this quiet note Levinas more or less admits that the olamic rapport with the Other is anything but equaled by the language of ethics; the rapport, in fact, is a *problem* for ethics to solve.

35. Maurice Blanchot, "The Narrative Voice," trans. Lydia Davis, in Sitney, ed., *Gaze of Orpheus,* pp. 133–44; idem, "The Narrative Voice," trans. Susan Hanson, in *The Infinite Conversation,* Theory and History of Literature ser. (Minneapolis: University of Minnesota Press, 1993), pp. 379–87; idem, "La voix narrative," in *L'entretien infini* (Paris: Gallimard, 1969), pp. 421–37.

36. This Other *(Autrui),* is, as we have been stressing, neither this one nor that one, neither an individual nor a group or crowd, but instead a singularity whose radical indifferentiation is the *other* of any representable difference.

37. Jean-Luc Nancy, "Of Being-in-Common," trans. James Creech, in *Community at Loose Ends,* ed. Miami Theory Collective (Minneapolis: University of Minnesota Press, 1991), pp. 1–12.

38. Blanchot, *Unavowable Community,* p. 8; idem, *La communauté inavouable,* p. 19.

39. Emmanuel Levinas, *Ethics and Infinity,* trans. Richard A. Cohen (Pittsburgh: Duquesne University Press, 1982), p. 86; idem, *Éthique et infini* (Paris: Librarie Arthème Fayard et Radio France, 1982), p. 80.

40. Blanchot, *Unavowable Community,* p. 11; idem, *La communauté inavouable,* p. 24.

41. Levinas, *Otherwise than Being or Beyond Essence,* p. 193 n. 1; idem, *Autrement qu'être ou au-delà de l'essence,* p. 125 n. 1.

42. Philippe Lacoue-Labarthe, "History and Mimesis," trans. Eduardo Cadava, in *Looking After Nietzsche,* ed. Laurence A. Ricklels (Albany: State University of New York Press, 1990), p. 229.

43. Quoted by Jacques Derrida in "Introduction: Desistance," trans. Christopher Fynsk, in Lacoue-Labarthe, *Typography*, p. 23.

Chapter Three. Blanchot, L'arrêt de mort, *and the Image of Literature*

1. Blanchot, "The Narrative Voice," trans. Davis, pp. 133–44; idem, "The Narrative Voice," trans. Hanson, pp. 379–87; idem, "La voix narrative," pp. 421–37.

2. Emmanuel Levinas, *Existence and Existents*, trans. Alphonso Lingis (The Hague: Martinus Nijhoff, 1978), pp. 52–64; idem, *De l'existence à l'existant* (Paris: Vrin, 1981), pp. 81–105.

3. Levinas, *Existence and Existents*, pp. 56–57; idem, *De l'existence à l'existant*, p. 91.

4. Levinas, *Existence and Existents*, p. 56; idem, *De l'existence à l'existant*, p. 91.

5. Levinas, *Existence and Existents*, p. 57; idem, *De l'existence à l'existant*, p. 91.

6. Agamben, *Coming Community*, pp. 53–58; idem, *La comunità che viene*, pp. 36–39.

7. Maurice Blanchot, "Characteristics of the Work of Art," trans. Ann Smock, in *Space of Literature*, p. 224; idem, "Les caractères de l'œuvre d'art," in *L'espace littéraire*, p. 297.

8. Blanchot, "Characteristics of the Work of Art," p. 223; idem, "Les caractères de l'œuvre d'art," p. 297.

9. Blanchot, "Characteristics of the Work of Art," p. 223; idem, "Les caractères de l'œuvre d'art," p. 296.

10. Blanchot, "Characteristics of the Work of Art," p. 223; idem, "Les caractères de l'œuvre d'art," p. 296.

11. Blanchot, "Characteristics of the Work of Art," p. 223; idem, "Les caractères de l'œuvre d'art," p. 297.

12. Levinas, *Existence and Existents*, p. 56; idem, *De l'existence à l'existant*, p. 90.

13. Levinas, *Existence and Existents*, p. 57; idem, *De l'existence à l'existant*, p. 92.

14. Levinas, *Existence and Existents*, p. 57; idem, *De l'existence à l'existant*, pp. 93–94.

15. Blanchot, "Two Versions of the Imaginary," trans. Davis, p. 79; idem, "The Two Versions of the Imaginary," trans. Smock, p. 254; idem, "Les deux versions de l'imaginaire," p. 341.

16. Jean-Luc Nancy, "Of Being-in-Common," trans. James Creech, in Miami Theory Collective, ed., *Community at Loose Ends*, p. 2.

17. Immanuel Kant, *Critique of Pure Reason*, trans. Norman Kemp Smith (New York: St. Martin's Press, 1965), p. 183.

18. Martin Heidegger, *Kant and the Problem of Metaphysics*, trans. James S. Churchill (Bloomington: Indiana University Press, 1962), pp. 102–6.

19. William J. Richardson, S.J., *Heidegger: Through Phenomenology to Thought* (The Hague: Martinus Nijhoff, 1963), p. 132.

20. Agamben, *Coming Community*, pp. 1–2; idem, *La comunità che viene*, pp. 3–4.

21. Agamben, *Coming Community*, pp. 53–56; idem, *La comunità che viene*, pp. 53–58.

22. Agamben, *Coming Community*, p. 76; idem, *La comunità che viene*, p. 52.

23. Maurice Blanchot, *Death Sentence*, trans. Lydia Davis (Barrytown, N.Y.: Station Hill Press, 1978), p. 31; idem, *L'arrêt de mort* (Paris: Gallimard, 1948), p. 54.

24. Levinas, *Otherwise than Being or Beyond Essence*, pp. 81–9; idem, *Autrement qu'être ou au-delà de l'essence*, pp. 102–13.

25. Blanchot, *Death Sentence*, p. 54; idem, *L'arrêt de mort*, p. 88.

26. Blanchot, *Death Sentence*, p. 54–55; idem, *L'arrêt de mort*, p. 89.

27. Levinas, *Otherwise than Being or Beyond Essence*, p. 111; idem, *Autrement qu'être ou au-delà de l'essence*, p. 141.

28. Blanchot, *Death Sentence*, p. 1; idem, *L'arrêt de mort*, p. 7.

29. Blanchot, *Death Sentence*, p. 46; idem, *L'arrêt de mort*, p. 76.

30. Blanchot, *Death Sentence*, p. 46; idem, *L'arrêt de mort*, p. 76.

31. Blanchot, *Death Sentence*, p. 46; idem, *L'arrêt de mort*, p. 76.

32. Blanchot, *Death Sentence*, p. 1; idem, *L'arrêt de mort*, p. 7.

33. Blanchot, *Death Sentence*, p. 2; idem, *L'arrêt de mort*, p. 8.

34. Levinas, "Reality and Its Shadow," p. 139; idem, "La réalité et son ombre," p. 784.

35. Marcel Proust, *Remembrance of Things Past*, trans. C. K. Scott Moncrieff and Terence Kilmartin (New York: Random House, 1981), 3:802.

36. Maurice Blanchot, *The Step Not Beyond*, trans. Lycette Nelson (Albany: State University of New York Press, 1992), p. 50; idem, *Le pas au-delà* (Paris: Gallimard 1973), p. 72.

37. Levinas, "The Servant and Her Master," p. 153; idem, "La servante et son maître," in *Sur Maurice Blanchot* (Montpellier: Fata Morgana, 1975), p. 34.

38. Blanchot, *Death Sentence*, p. 79; idem, *L'arrêt de mort*, p. 126.

39. Blanchot, *Death Sentence*, p. 81.

40. Maurice Blanchot, "Reading," trans. Lydia Davis, in *Gaze of Orpheus*, pp. 94–96; idem, "Reading," trans. Ann Smock, in *Space of Literature*, pp. 194–96; idem, "Lire," in *L'espace littéraire*, pp. 256–58.

41. Steven Shaviro, *Passion and Excess: Blanchot, Bataille, and Literary Theory* (Tallahassee: The Florida State University Press, 1990), pp. 142–43.

42. Blanchot, *Step Not Beyond*, p. 50; idem, *Le pas au-delà*, p. 72.

43. Shaviro, *Passion and Excess*, pp. 142–43.

44. Blanchot, *Death Sentence*, p. 79; idem, *L'arrêt de mort*, p. 126.

45. Blanchot, *Death Sentence*, p. 79; idem, *L'arrêt de mort*, 127.

46. Blanchot, *Death Sentence*, p. 80; idem, *L'arrêt de mort*, p. 127.

47. Maurice Blanchot, "Kafka and the Work's Demand," trans. Ann Smock, in *Space of Literature*, p. 57–83; idem, "Kafka et l'exigence de l'œuvre," in *L'espace littèraire*, pp. 59–98.

48. Blanchot, *Death Sentence*, p. 32; idem, *L'arrêt de mort*, p. 55.

49. Blanchot, *Death Sentence*, p. 72; idem, *L'arrêt de mort*, p. 115.

50. Blanchot, *Death Sentence*, p. 72; idem, *L'arrêt de mort*, p. 116.

51. Blanchot, *Death Sentence*, p. 79; idem, *L'arrêt de mort*, p. 126.

52. Agamben, *Coming Community*, p. 84; idem, *La comunità che viene*, p. 58.

53. Agamben, *Coming Community*, p. 84; idem, *La comunità che viene*, p. 58.

54. Blanchot, *Step Not Beyond*, p. 93; idem, *Le pas au-delà*, p. 129.

55. Levinas, "Reality and Its Shadow," p. 140; idem, "La réalité et son ombre," p. 785.

56. Levinas, *Otherwise than Being or Beyond Essence*, p. 199 n. 21; idem, *Autrement qu'être ou au-delà de l'essence*, p. 191 n. 21.

57. P. Adams Sitney makes this observation in his afterword to Blanchot, *Gaze of Orpheus*, p. 171.

58. Shaviro, *Passion and Excess*, pp. 142–70.

59. Blanchot, *Death Sentence*, p. 20; idem, *L'arrêt de mort*, p. 30.

60. Foucault, "Maurice Blanchot," p. 39.

61. Blanchot, *Death Sentence*, p. 30; idem, *L'arrêt de mort*, p. 52–53.

62. Blanchot, *Death Sentence*, p. 20; idem, *L'arrêt de mort*, p. 35.

63. Blanchot, *Death Sentence*, p. 20; idem, *L'arrêt de mort*, p. 36.

64. Blanchot, *Death Sentence*, p. 81.

65. Levinas, "The Servant and Her Master," p. 155; idem, "La servante et son maître," p. 37.

66. Levinas, "The Servant and Her Master," p. 155; idem, "La servante et son maître," p. 37.

67. Levinas, "The Servant and Her Master," p. 155; idem, "La servante et son maître," p. 37.

68. Levinas, "The Servant and Her Master," p. 155; idem, "La servante et son maître," p. 37.

69. Levinas, "The Servant and Her Master," p. 157; idem, "La servante et son maître," p. 40.

70. Levinas, "The Servant and Her Master," p. 157; idem, "La servante et son maître," p. 40.

71. Levinas, "The Servant and Her Master," p. 157; idem, "La servante et son maître," p. 40.

72. Agamben, *Coming Community*, p. 104; idem, *La comunità che viene*, p. 77.

73. Blanchot, "The Outside, the Night," p. 163–70; idem, "La dehors, la nuit," pp. 213–24.

74. Blanchot, "Characteristics of the Work of Art," pp. 232; idem, "Les caractères de l'œuvre d'art," pp. 310.

75. Levinas, *Otherwise than Being or Beyond Essence*, p. 104 and 106; idem, *Autrement qu'être ou au-delà de l'essence*, pp. 132–33 and 135.

76. Blanchot, "Characteristics of the Work of Art," pp. 232–33; idem, "Les caractères de l'œuvre d'art," p. 310.

77. Blanchot, "Characteristics of the Work of Art," p. 233; idem, "Les caractères de l'œuvre d'art," p. 311.

78. Blanchot, *Death Sentence*, p. 20; idem, *L'arrêt de mort*, p. 35.

79. Blanchot, "Two Versions of the Imaginary," trans. Davis, p. 87; idem, "The Two Versions of the Imaginary," trans. Smock, pp. 261–62; idem, "Les deux versions de l'imaginaire," p. 352.

80. "The dead present is the impossibility of realizing a presence—an impossibility that is present, that is there as that which doubles every present, the shadow of the present, which the present carries and hides in itself. When I am alone, in this present, I am not alone, but am already returning to myself in the form of Someone. Someone is there, when I am alone. [Le présent mort est l'impossibilité de réaliser une présence, impossibilité qui est présente, qui est là comme ce qui double tout présent, l'ombre du présent, que celui-ci porte et dissimule en lui. Quand je suis seul, je ne suis pas seul, mais, dans ce présent, je reviens déjà à moi sous la forme de Quelqu'un.

Quelqu'un est là, où je suis seul.]" Maurice Blanchot, "The Essential Solitude," trans. Lydia Davis, in *Gaze of Orpheus*, p. 74; idem, "The Essential Solitude," trans. Ann Smock, in *Space of Literature*, p. 31; idem, "La solitude essentielle," in *L'espace littéraire*, p. 27.

81. Blanchot, *Death Sentence*, p. 32; idem, *L'arrêt de mort*, pp. 55–56.

82. Blanchot, "Characteristics of the Work of Art," p. 232; idem, "Les caractères de l'œuvre d'art," p. 310.

Chapter Four. Agamben and the Political Neuter

1. Blanchot, "The Essential Solitude," trans. Davis, p. 69; idem, "The Essential Solitude," trans. Smock, pp. 26–27; idem, "La solitude essentielle," p. 21.

2. Blanchot, "The Essential Solitude," trans. Davis, p. 69; idem, "The Essential Solitude," trans. Smock, p. 27; idem, "La solitude essentielle," p. 17.

3. Blanchot, "The Essential Solitude," trans. Davis, p. 77; idem, "The Essential Solitude," trans. Smock, p. 33; idem, "La solitude essentielle," pp. 27–28.

4. Blanchot, "The Essential Solitude," trans. Davis, p. 74; idem, "The Essential Solitude," trans. Smock, p. 31; idem, "La solitude essentielle," p. 24.

5. Mikkel Borch-Jacobsen, "Hypnosis in Psychoanalysis," trans. Angela Brewer and X. P. Callahan, in *Emotional Tie*, p. 50.

6. On the relation between analysis, hysteria and narrative modes see ibid., p. 184 n. 14.

7. Ibid., pp. 49–62.

8. Lacoue-Labarthe, "Typography," p. 133.

9. Blanchot, "Two Versions of the Imaginary," trans. Davis, p. 88; idem, "The Two Versions of the Imaginary," trans. Smock, p. 262; idem, "Les deux versions de l'imaginaire," p. 352.

10. Levinas, *Existence and Existents*, p. 56; idem, *De l'existence à l'existant*, p. 90.

11. Levinas, *Existence and Existents*, p. 56; idem, *De l'existence à l'existant*, p. 90.

12. Antonin Artaud, "Exposition Balthus à la Gallerie Pierre," *La Nouvelle Revue Français* 22, no. 248 (May 1934): 899–90.

13. Agamben, *Coming Community*, p. 89; idem, *La comunità che viene*, p. 62.

14. Translator's note in Agamben, *Coming Community*, p. 107.

15. Jean-Paul Sartre, *The Transcendence of the Ego*, trans. Forrest Williams and Robert Kirkpatrick (New York: Hill and Wang, 1990).

16. Agamben, *Coming Community*, pp. 66–67; idem, *La comunità che viene*, pp. 45–46.

17. Blanchot, "Two Versions of the Imaginary," p. 85; idem, "The Two Versions of the Imaginary," p. 260; idem, "Les deux versions de l'imaginaire," p. 350.

18. Agamben, *Coming Community*, pp. 19–20; idem, *La comunità che viene*, pp. 15–16.

19. Agamben, *Coming Community*, p. 19; idem, *La comunità che viene*, p. 15.

20. Agamben, *Coming Community*, p. 11; idem, *La comunità che viene*, pp. 8–9.

21. Agamben, *Coming Community*, p. 85; idem, *La comunità che viene*, p. 58

22. Agamben, *Coming Community*, pp. 79–83; idem, *La comunità che viene*, pp. 53–57. Let us emphasize yet again the neutrality of this "one" who speaks. It is not simply the experience that *I* speak, but rather that the "I speak" is neutralized such that it is experienced as an anonymous entry into language. As it enters language, the individual identity "I" is overwhelmed and carried away by language, or, more simply, by speaking.

23. Blanchot, *Death Sentence*, pp. 61–63; idem, *L'arrêt de mort*, pp. 99–103.

24. Giorgio Agamben, *Language and Death: The Place of Negativity*, trans. Karen E. Pinkus with Michael Hardt, Theory and History of Literature ser. (Minneapolis: University of Minnesota Press, 1991), pp. 84–98; idem, *Il linguaggio e la morte: Un seminario sul luogo della negatività* (Torino: Giulio Einaudi Editore, 1982), pp. 104–23.

25. Agamben, *Language and Death*, pp. 94–95; idem, *Il linguaggio e la morte*, pp. 118–20.

26. Agamben, *Language and Death*, pp. 63–65; idem, *Il linguaggio e la morte*, pp. 79–81.

27. Agamben, *Coming Community*, p. 82; idem, *La comunità che viene*, p. 56.

28. Agamben, *Language and Death*, pp. 96–106; idem, *Il linguaggio e la morte*, pp. 121–33. Proper attention to this highly important book would require its own chapter. We simply wish to retain from this book Agamben's drive to think community (human being) outside negativity, negative presentation, or negative theology. He is critical of Blanchot's *La communauté inavouable* for retaining too negative a language. It is a part of our effort here to show that what Blanchot will describe as an "inability to say I," Agamben will describe as an "ability to not say I." That is, his *La comunità che viene* answers the promise of an "infancy of the human" that concludes *Il linguaggio e la morte* by nuancing Blanchotian anonymity toward a latent, ambiguous, and radical potential.

29. Agamben, *Language and Death*, p. 94; idem, *Il linguaggio e la morte*, p. 118 (italics in original).

30. Agamben, *Coming Community*, pp. 96–97. (According to a private conversation with Agemben's translator, the parenthetical passage from which this quotation is taken appears only in the French and English editions of the text.)

31. Levinas, "Reality and Its Shadow," p. 135; idem, "La réalité et son ombre," p. 777.

32. Agamben, *Coming Community*, p. 101; idem, *La comunità che viene*, p. 73 (italics in original).

33. Agamben, *Coming Community*, pp. 76–77; idem, *La comunità che viene*, pp. 51–52. Agamben understands the Idea as that "halo," or supplement, or pre-scriptive image, that para-exists in the empty space of "all its predicates." Like Levinas and Blanchot, he understands the concept to refer to being as it is grasped in its intelligibility within the horizons of a world.

34. Agamben, *Coming Community*, p. 89; idem, *La comunità che viene*, p. 62.

35. Heidegger, *Kant and the Problem of Metaphysics*, pp. 102–6.

36. Ibid., p. 113–14.

37. Blanchot, "Two Versions of the Imaginary," trans. Davis, p. 87; idem, "The Two Versions of the Imaginary," trans. Smock, pp. 261–62; idem, "Les deux versions de l'imaginaire," 356.

38. Richardson, *Heidegger,* pp. 107ff., in the pages that follow we will reproduce the architecture of Richardson's summary of the *Kantbuch*, highlighting those aspects that intersect with our interest in Agamben, and departing from Richardson only to quote either Heidegger's or Kant's own words in order to more rigorously specify the notions that interest us.

39. Kant, *Critique of Pure Reason*, p. 269.

40. Heidegger, *Kant and the Problem of Metaphysics*, p. 36 n. 17.

41. Ibid., p. 37 (italics in original).

42. Kant, *Critique of Pure Reason*, p. 84.

43. Ibid., p. 181.

44. Heidegger, *Kant and the Problem of Metaphysics*, pp. 102–6 [italics in original].

45. Agamben, *Coming Community*, pp. 9–12; idem, *La comunità che viene*, pp. 7–9.

46. Richardson, *Heidegger,* p. 131.

47. Ibid., p. 131.

48. Agamben, *Coming Community*, p. 77; idem, *La comunità che viene*, p. 52 (italics in original).

49. Richardson, *Heidegger,* p. 132.

50. Agamben, *Coming Community*, p. 10; idem, *La comunità che viene*, p. 8 (italics in original).

51. Kant, *Critique of Pure Reason*, p. 137.

52. Heidegger, *Kant and the Problem of Metaphysics*, p. 127.

53. Martin Heidegger, "Brief über den Humanismus," in *Wegmarken* (Frankfurt: Vittorio Klostermann, 1976), p. 359.

54. Richardson, *Heidegger,* p. 152.

55. Immanuel Kant, *Opus posthumum*, trans. Eckart Förster and Michael Rosen (Cambridge: Cambridge University Press, 1993), p. 172.

56. Richardson, *Heidegger,* p. 154.

57. Agamben, *Coming Community*, p. 103; idem, *La comunità che viene*, p. 75.

58. Agamben, *Coming Community*, p. 76; idem, *La comunità che viene*, p. 52 [italics in original].

59. Agamben, *Coming Community*, p. 11; idem, *La comunità che viene*, p. 9.

60. Agamben, *Coming Community*, p. 11; idem, *La comunità che viene*, pp. 8–9.

61. Blanchot, "The Essential Solitude," trans. Davis, p. 69; idem, "The Essential Solitude," trans. Smock, p. 26; idem, "La solitude essentielle," p. 17.

62. Agamben, *Coming Community*, p. 82; idem, *La comunità che viene*, p. 56.

63. Agamben, *Coming Community*, p. 82; idem, *La comunità che viene*, p. 56.

64. Agamben, *Coming Community*, p. 79; idem, *La comunità che viene*. p. 53.

65. Borch-Jacobsen, "The Freudian Subject," p. 35.

66. Agamben, *Coming Community*, p. 50; idem, *La comunità che viene*, p. 35.

67. Quoted by Giorgio Agamben in *Infancy and History: Essays on the Destruction of Experience*, trans. Liz Heron (London: Verso, 1993), pp. 31–32; idem, *Infanzia e storia: Distruzione dell'esperienza e origine della storia* (Torino: Giulio Einaudi Editore, 1978), p 27.

68. Agamben, *Infancy and History*, p. 44; idem, *Infanzia e storia*, pp. 41–42.

69. Quoted in Agamben, *Infancy and History*, p. 44; idem, *Infanzia e storia*, p. 41.

70. Quoted in Agamben, *Infancy and History*, p. 45; idem, *Infanzia e storia*, p. 43.

71. Agamben, *Infancy and History*, p. 46; idem, *Infanzia e storia*, pp. 43–44.

72. Martin Heidegger, *Being and Time*, trans. John Macquarrie and Edward Robinson (New York: Harper and Row, 1962), pp. 149–219.

73. Quoted in Agamben, *Infancy and History,* p. 46; idem, *Infanzia e storia,* p. 44.

74. Blanchot, "The Essential Solitude," trans. Davis, pp. 63–77; idem, "The Essential Solitude," trans. Smock, pp. 21–34; idem, "La solitude essentielle," pp. 13–32.

75. Levinas, *Existence and Existents,* p. 63 n. 7; idem, *De l'existence à l'existant,* p. 103 n. 1.

Selected Bibliography

Agamben, Giorgio. *The Coming Community*. Translated by
Michael Hardt. Theory Out of Bounds ser. Minneapolis:
University of Minnesota Press, 1993.

———. *La comunità che viene*. Torino: Giulio Einaudi Editore,
1990.

———. *Infancy and History: Essays on the Destruction of
Experience*. Translated by Liz Heron. London: Verso, 1993.

———. *Infanzia e storia: Distruzione dell'esperienza e origine
della storia*. Torino: Giulio Einaudi Editore, 1978.

———. *Language and Death: The Place of Negativity*. Translated
by Karen Pinkus with Michael Hardt. Theory and History of
Literature ser. Minneapolis: University of Minnesota Press,
1991.

———. *Il linguaggio e la morte: Un seminario sul luogo della
negatività*. Torino: Giulio Einaudi Editore, 1982.

Artaud, Antonin. "Exposition Balthus à la Gallerie Pierre." *La
Nouvelle Revue Francais* 22, no. 248 (May 1934).

Bataille, Georges. *The Tears of Eros*. Translated by Peter Connor.
San Francisco: City Lights Books, 1989.

Blanchot, Maurice. *L'arrêt de mort*. L'imaginaire ser. Paris:
Gallimard, 1971.

———. *La communauté inavouable*. Paris: Les Éditions Minuit, 1983.

———. *Death Sentence*. Translated by Lydia Davis. Barrytown, N.Y.: Station Hill Press, 1978.

———. *L'espace littéraire*. Idées ser. Paris: Gallimard, 1955.

———. *The Gaze of Orpheus*. Translated by Lydia Davis. Barrytown, N.Y.: Station Hill Press, 1981.

———. *The Infinite Conversation*. Translated by Susan Hanson. Theory and History of Literature ser. Minneapolis: University of Minnesota Press, 1993.

———. *Le livre à venir*. Idées ser. Paris: Gallimard, 1971.

———. *The Space of Literature*. Translated by Ann Smock. Lincoln: University of Nebraska Press, 1982.

———. *The Step Not Beyond*. Translated by Lycette Nelson. Albany: State University of New York Press, 1992.

———. *Thomas the Obscure*. Translated by Robert Lamberton. Barrytown, N.Y.: Station Hill Press, 1988.

———. *The Unavowable Community*. Translated by Pierre Joris. Barrytown, N.Y.: Station Hill Press, 1988.

———. *When the Time Comes*. Translated by Lydia Davis. Barrytown, N.Y.: Station Hill Press.

Borch-Jacobsen, Mikkel. "Écoute." *Poésie* 35 (1986).

———. *The Emotional Tie: Psychoanalysis, Mimesis, and Affect*. Translated by Douglas Brick et al. Stanford, Calif.: Stanford University Press.

———. *The Freudian Subject*. Translated by Douglas Brick. Stanford, Calif.: Stanford University Press, 1988.

Derrida, Jacques. "At this moment in this work here I am." Translated by Ruben Berezdivin. In *Re-reading Levinas,* edited by Robert Bernasoni and Simon Critchley. Bloomington: Indiana University Press, 1991.

———. *Of Grammatology*. Translated by Gayatri Chakravorty Spivak. Baltimore: The Johns Hopkins University Press, 1976.

Flesch, William. "Proximity and Power: Shakespearean and Dramatic Space." *Theater Journal* 39, no. 3 (October 1987).

————. "Posthumous Sadness." Unpublished paper.

Foucault, Michel. *Maurice Blanchot: The Thought from Outside,* translated by Brian Massumi. In *Foucault/Blanchot.* New York: Zone Books, 1987.

Heidegger, Martin. *Being and Time.* Translated by John Macquarrie and Edward Robinson. New York: Harper and Row, 1962.

————. "Brief über den Humanismus." In *Wegmarken.* Frankfurt: Vittorio Klostermann, 1976.

————. *Kant and the Problem of Metaphysics.* Translated by James S. Churchill. Bloomington: Indiana University Press, 1962.

————. "Letter on Humanism." In *Basic Writings,* translated by David Farrell Krell. New York: Harper and Row, 1977.

————. *Nihilism.* Vol. 4 of *Nietzsche,* translated by David Farrell Krell. San Francisco: Harper and Row, 1982.

————. *Poetry, Language, Thought.* Translated by Albert Hofstadter. New York: Harper and Row, 1971.

Kant, Immanuel. *Critique of Pure Reason.* Translated by Norman Kemp Smith. New York: St. Martin's Press, 1965.

————. *Opus posthumum.* Translated by Eckart Förster and Michael Rosen. Cambridge: Cambridge University Press, 1993.

Lacoue-Labarthe, Philippe. "Catastrophe," translated by Andrea Tarnowski. In *Word Traces,* edited by Aris Fioretos. Baltimore: The Johns Hopkins University Press, 1994.

————. *Heidegger, Art and Politics.* Translated by Chris Turner. Cambridge: Basil Blackwell, 1990.

————. "History and Mimesis," translated by Eduardo Cadava. In *Looking After Nietzsche,* edited by Laurence A. Rickels. Albany: State University of New York Press, 1990.

————. *Typography: Mimesis, Philosophy, Politics.* Edited by Christopher Fynsk. Cambridge: Harvard University Press, 1989.

Levinas, Emmanuel. *Autrement qu'être ou au-delà de l'essence.* The Hague: Martinus Nijhoff, 1974.

———. "Being and the Other: On Paul Celan," translated by Steven Melville. *Chicago Review* 29, nos. 16-21 (winter, 1978).

———. *De Dieu qui vient à l'idée.* Paris: Vrin, 1982.

———. *De l'existence à l'existant.* Paris: Vrin, 1973.

———. *Ethics and Infinity.* Translated by Richard A. Cohen. Pittsburgh: Duquesne University Press, 1985.

———. *Éthique et Infini.* Paris: Librairie Arthème Fayard et Radio-France, 1982.

———. *Existence and Existents.* Translated by Alphonso Lingis. The Hague: Martinus Nijhoff, 1978.

———. *Face to Face with Levinas.* Edited by Richard A. Cohen. Albany: State University of New York Press, 1986.

———. *The Levinas Reader.* Edited by Seán Hand. Cambridge: Basil Balckwell, 1989.

———. *Otherwise Than Being or Beyond Essence.* Translated by Alphonso Lingis. The Hague: Martinus Nijhoff, 1981.

———. "Philosophy and Awakening," translated by Mary Quaintance. In *Who Comes After the Subject?,* edited by Eduardo Cadava, Peter Connor, and Jean-Luc Nancy. New York: Routledge, 1991.

———. "La réalité et son ombre." *Les Temps Modernes* 4, no. 38 (November 1948).

———. *Sur Maurice Blanchot.* Montpellier: Fata Morgana, 1975.

———. *Totalité et Infini.* The Hague: Martinus Nujhoff, 1961.

———. *Totality and Infinity.* Translated by Alphonso Lingis. Pittsburgh: Duquesne University Press, 1969.

Libertson, Joseph. *Proximity: Levinas, Blanchot, Bataille: Communication.* The Hague: Martinus Nijhoff, 1982.

Llewelyn, John. "Levinas, Derrida and Others *Vis-à-vis.*" In *The Provocation of Levinas,* edited by Robert Bernasconi and David Wood. New York: Routledge, 1988.

Nancy, Jean-Luc. *The Inoperative Community.* Translated by Peter Connor, Lisa Garbus, Michael Holland, and Simona Sawhney. Theory and History of Literature ser. Minneapolis: University of Minnesota Press 1991.

———. "Of Being-in-Common," translated by James Creech. In *Community at Loose Ends*, edited by Miami Theory Collective. Minneapolis: University of Minnesota Press, 1991.

Nancy, Jean-Luc, and Philippe Lacoue-Labarthe. *The Title of the Letter.* Translated by François Raffoul and David Pettigrew. Albany: State University of New York Press, 1992.

Proust, Marcel. *Remembrance of Things Past.* Translated by C. K. Scott Moncrieff and Terence Kilmartin. New York: Random House, 1981.

Richardson, William J., S.J. *Heidegger: Through Phenomenology to Thought.* The Hague: Martinus Nijhoff, 1963.

Sartre, Jean-Paul. *The Transcendence of the Ego.* Translated by Forrest Williams and Robert Kirkpatrick. New York: Hill and Wang, 1990.

Shaviro, Steven. *Passion and Excess: Blanchot, Bataille, and Literary Theory.* Tallahasee: The Florida State University Press, 1990.

Wittgenstein, Ludwig. *Philosophical Investigations.* Translated by G. E. M. Anscombe. New York: Macmillan, 1968.

———. *Tractatus Logico-Philosophicus.* Translated by D. F. Pears and B. F. McGuinness. London: Routledge and Kegan Paul, 1961.

Index